THE SUNDAY HOMILY

SCRIPTURAL
AND
LITURGICAL
RENEWAL

Edited by
John Burke, O.P.

Nihil Obstat:

Rev. A. D. Lee, O.P.
Censor Deputatus

Imprimatur:

† Patrick A. O'Boyle
Archbishop of Washington

June 10, 1966

Library of Congress Catalog Card Number
66-26068

Copyright 1966
THE THOMIST PRESS

CONTENTS

PART II
REPORTS FROM THE RAPPORTEURS

PREFACE

This volume contains papers delivered at the 1965 Workshop on the Renewal in Scriptural and Liturgical Preaching. Conducted under the joint sponsorship of the School of Sacred Theology and the Speech and Drama Department of The Catholic University of America, the workshop was directed towards helping the parish priest preach his Sunday homilies in the spirit of renewal envisioned by the Second Vatican Council.

The workshop centered around small group sessions in the writing and delivery of homilies under the guidance of professional teachers of speech and homiletics acting as *rapporteurs*. In these small group sessions all the participants were able to give at least three homilies before an audience of fellow priests of similar age, experience, and position. The *rapporteurs* led their groups in candid evaluations of the homilies given, with special attention being directed to the relevancy of their content to the lives and needs of the audience, as well as to the vividness and concreteness of the language in which they were expressed. Furthermore, all the participants were able to video-tape a two-minute sermonette for self-criticism at a local television station. The reactions of the *rapporteurs* to these sessions are an important second part of this book.

To enable the priest-participants to make the best use of these small group meetings, background lecture-discussion periods on liturgy and Scripture, as well as other sciences and arts which contribute to effective preaching were held each morning of the workshop. The papers delivered in these periods constitute the first and major portion of this book.

THE ELEMENTS OF COMMUNICATION

The word "communication" means "the sharing of truth," and this sharing of truth necessarily involves four elements: first, a speaker;

secondly, the speaker's message; thirdly, the audience to whom the message is directed; and finally, the vocal symbols by which the message is communicated. The preacher must be aware of the contribution that each one of these elements makes towards his finished product—the effective homily.

THE SPEAKER

The first paper, by Mr. William H. Graham, outlines ways in which the preacher can develop his preaching potential by describing how his mind, emotions, body and voice can be formed into more perfect instruments through which the Word of God may be shared with others.

The second paper, by the Reverend Richard T. Hanley, considers the preacher as one sent by the Church to be official minister of the Word of God. Father Hanley discusses the nature of the office of preaching, its importance, and its purpose in the life of the Church. Since preaching holds first place in the apostolate, it is hoped that priests will become more aware of the great dignity which belongs to them in their office of preacher.

THE MESSAGE

The second element in communication is the message. The preacher's message, that is to say the content of his preaching, is provided for him by the Church, and it is nothing less than divine revelation. Four papers are concerned with the message.

Monsignor John J. Cassels writes on the liturgical relations of the homily, showing how it fits into the liturgical action of the Mass. He concerns himself especially with the *Constitution on the Liturgy* of the Second Vatican Council, and by analyzing its contents shows the scope of the freedom given to the preacher in determining what he shall preach as well as the manner in which he does it. At the same time, Monsignor Cassels gives guidelines for the structure of homilies, and recalls the decrees of the Council of Trent relative to the pastor's responsibility for preaching the entire conspectus of Christian doctrine.

The three papers on Scripture are integrally related. In the first, Father Richard Kugelman gives a general introduction to Scripture as a practical source of preaching. He explicates the difference as well as the intimate relationship between preaching and exegesis of Scriptural texts, and indicates Scripture's own injunctions to preachers on how to preach. The senses of Scripture and the place of the Old Testament in Christian preaching are also discussed. He concludes with some practical norms to guide the preacher in his use of Scripture in modern preaching.

In the second paper on Scripture, Father Alan Smith comments on it as a history of salvation, showing in particular the significance of the sacred events as they relate to the lives of Christians today. In agreement with R. G. Collingwood's dictum, "History proper is the history of thought. There are no mere events in history," Father Smith considers sacred history not as a record of isolated facts, but as the events which reveal God's loving thought towards us. Within the general framework of salvation history, he also treats of the notion of *kerygma* and makes particular reference to the place of the parables in preaching Sacred Scripture.

The last paper on Scripture is by Father Geoffrey Wood who outlines particular themes in the Scriptures which provide a fruitful source and approach to preaching. He gives great importance to the People of God theme in preaching, and indicates how it can be effectively used to increase the motive power of religion among Christians today.

THE AUDIENCE

The element in communication to which all the others are ordered is the audience. We must ask, therefore, what are the current needs of Christian people? In spite of good content, and logical organization, a homily may not be effective simply because it in no way touches the lives of the people to whom it is preached. The preacher may depend solely on aspects of the spiritual life which he has come across in his reading, has found of tremendous value to himself, and thinks would be suitable for all his people without investigating more completely the actual situation. On the other hand, a pastor may be so caught up with some surface problem of his parish that he forgets the underlying and more subtle forces which are at work in his parishoners' lives, and of which even they themselves are not aware. Philosophy and sociology assist the preacher to understand those influences which are profoundly forming today's audiences and, consequently, determining how they will receive the message of Christ when it is preached to them.

Since naturalism is the prevailing philosophy of our times, Father Robert Paul Mohan's paper on the influence of naturalism on contemporary social goals is of special value. Our society has a naturalistic view of what constitutes happiness and the full human life—a view which in many ways is opposed to the gospel. Still, it determines to a greater or lesser degree what modern Christians want out of life. This paper explains what difficulties naturalism presents to the preacher's efforts to change the lives of his present-day hearers.

In addition, since his audiences are formed by their families as well as by society, the preacher should have a rather complete insight into modern family life. Specifically, he should know what a pluralistic, democratic society expects of the father and mother, since this expectation will usually be realized even in Christian homes. Monsignor

Christopher Knott investigates the modern American family, especially the parental roles and their influence on the reception of Christ's gospel.

By a fuller understanding of social and familial factors affecting the members of a modern congregation, it is hoped that the pastor-preacher will be better able to make his homilies relevant to the lives of his listeners, disposing them for a truly Christian response to the Good News of Salvation.

THE SYMBOLS

Professor Leo Brady in the last paper discusses techniques of creative writing which can be used by the ordinary preacher. Like the poet, the preacher is a creative artist. While the poet contemplates nature, and expresses what he experiences there in a poem, the preacher contemplates Scripture and the liturgy, and expresses his experience of God who is revealed there in a homily. Contemplation, experience, expression—the activity of the artist. Professor Brady shows how the methods of the natural artist can be of great benefit to the supernatural artist in the preparation of his homilies.

In conclusion, I wish to acknowledge my indebtedness to the Very Reverend Walter J. Schmitz, S.S., Dean of the School of Sacred Theology, and the Reverend Gilbert V. Hartke, O.P., Head of the Speech and Drama Department of The Catholic University of America whose generous and dedicated response to Archbishop Patrick A. O'Boyle's request for a workshop on preaching made this cooperative project possible.

JOHN BURKE, O.P.
Director of the Workshop

PART I
PRESENTATION
OF
MAIN TOPICS

THE THEORY OF COMMUNICATION

by

William H. Graham

We all have crosses to bear. Most of them, with the help of God, we count as blessings. The others we call challenges. And I would guess that high on the list of modern challenges to the serenity of the priestly life must be that phenomenon known, in groundhog terms, as the emerging layman. The priest finds him poking his head through rectory windows and jamming his foot in the doorways, always with a smile, offering his expertise to solve parish problems. If you look under the pastor's desk you'll probably find one ready to say, "Father, if you don't mind my saying so, I'd like to make a suggestion. I think you ought to do it this way." Well, here he is again, Helpful Hank, the emerging layman, standing before the priest to get his two cents in. And yet I stand not as an expert but as a listener. And I speak as one less inclined to tell the clergy what they need to do than to tell them what I need to hear.

We laymen have an increasingly sophisticated understanding of the role of the Church in the world and of the apostolate of every Christian. Many of us can speak in impressive tones of sincere concern about the great problem of leading a truly Christian life in a materialistic society. We can, and unfortunately we often do, discuss the institution of the Church in the same terms and with the same limited vision we apply to an analysis of a department of the federal government.

We have a neat trick of closing our eyes to the absence of zeal and perfect charity in our own lives while looking for and concentrating on the human weaknesses and deficiencies in the lives of others.

3

We find fault with our priests. We say they do not understand us; the complexities and problems we face, or our needs. We detach ourselves from their instruction and guidance by claiming that priests live in another world with no mortgage to meet, no mouths to feed or children to clothe, and that they just don't speak our language. Why is it so? The priest knows he loves. Why can't the layman see it? Why can't he hear it? Why can't he feel it? What is blocking the communication of the Word?

Well, it may be that the layman doesn't really want to listen to the Word. It may be that he mouthes his gripes and grievances out of a subconscious urge to throw up a barricade against the Hound of Heaven. But it may also be that the Word is not being spoken with the fire of love. It may be that the instrument of the Word, the person of the priest, is not operating at one hundred per cent of his capacity. This paper is an occasion to question the equipment; to polish the reliable old parts and to replace the bad parts.

We have no need here of stressing the importance of communicating the Word of God to all people. The priestly life is dedicated to that mission. The voice of Christ speaks through the voice of the Church and the voice of the Church speaks through every priest in every church throughout the world. So our purpose here is directed to one end:—that the Word may be heard—and heard not only through the layman's ears but in his mind and heart. The immediate need is this: that the clergy develop more fully their potential to preach the Word of God; to cultivate their minds, emotions, bodies, and voices as more perfect instruments through which the Word of God may be shared with others. A simply enough stated objective. What are the problems?

First we have to admit that such a need exists and, if we do admit it, then we must meet that need. Can we admit that the Christian community, assembled to offer the Holy Sacrifice of the Mass, is seldom a community of spirit? Can we admit that at moments of communication between priest and people there is seldom a union of minds and hearts? I think we can. This is the need: to bring about a communion of souls among the members of the Mystical Body of Christ. In order to meet this need, both priests and people must want to move more closely together, must want to move towards each other in Christ. The concentration here will be on what the clergy can do to encourage this more perfect union. But there are obstacles and they must be overcome. There are misconceptions which impede development of the priest as an instrument of communication. There are bad habits of communication which have become so much a part of clerical presentation that priests may think of them as natural. Therefore, we direct the following observations to the priests who are victimized by these obstacles.

MISCONCEPTIONS

The first misconception which I would like to discuss is the one about the average man. The 'average man' concept prevails rather strongly in our society. It's "You gotta be one of the boys to have the common touch." It influences human beings who enter the seminary and are ordained priests. And it results in much preaching that is reduced to the casual and insignificant because it is the kind of preaching which is designed and delivered in such a way as not to offend; not to alienate; not to appear phony or artificial. It is based on a negative. But, since the content of the gospel or a sermon is extraordinarily and eternally significant, the communication of that content requires an extraordinary use of self. Not some other self but the self of the communicator. But because of this "let's be our natural selves" approach which translates into average, casual, dull selves, there are many sermons being preached today with inspiring content and expiring delivery.

The second misconception regards training in techniques of oral communication as unnatural and artificial. The principle here is this: an effective technique of oral communication does not show itself separate from the thing to be communicated, from the material. The training of the voice and the body should result in the recognition that these are the means of touching human hearts and minds and guiding immortal souls. The movement of the voice and body must not be regarded as a representation or demonstration of an idea but rather an extension, and therefore a vital part, of the idea. Without the extension of the idea into the body and the voice of the communicator it is not likely that it will be completely shared. Therefore, the development of technique in oral communication means the cultivation of the capacity to share. At the moment of sharing the total concentration must be on the listener's understanding and response and not on how it looks or how it sounds.

The third misconception is that when preaching or reading the gospel it is necessary to appear and sound priest-like, which is ridiculous. The priesthood has no specific size, shape, sound, or style. Did Pope John look like Pope Paul? Is it likely that St. Peter sounded like St. Paul? Aren't they all priest-like? If you have been harboring one of these misconceptions, they have prevented you from developing your capacity as a human being to communicate the Word of God. If you have been concerned with preserving the image of the priesthood by attempting to appear and sound priestlike, by trying to be humble, intelligent, noble, or whatever other words you use to describe the ideal priest, you have been cutting off your specific personal capacity to communicate through your unique individual voice and body.

On the other hand, you may not have been harboring any of these misconceptions. You may never have attempted to reduce yourself to an average man. You may have always recognized the importance of technique in clear and effective communication. And you may never have concerned yourself with trying to be priest-like in an abstract way. Nevertheless, there may be and probably are some habits which limit your effectiveness. I only want to point out a few of these in an effort to illustrate how much of an obstacle a bad habit can be.

BAD HABITS

Some of these bad habits creep in as a result of one of those three misconceptions or some unique misconception that may be identified as peculiarly your own. The habits of the voice and body, if they are not in happy union with the workings of the mind and heart of the communicator, can greatly reduce the possibility of effective communication. In other words, your good intentions and your willing heart must, as a communicator, be united in a vital bond with a live and flexible voice working together towards the senses as well as the souls of the listener.

What are some of the habits of the body? I'm sure you have observed, in others, a habit of lifelessness which I can only suppose comes out of some public image concept of the way one must behave when talking about loving Christ. That's the body that stands there with not a ripple of activity in any of its muscles. Now it may be that the mind is working very actively. It may be. But I guarantee you that that congregation sits there and doubts that the being is fully alive. Should you ask him why he stands this way he will tell you he is not an actor; he is not going to be histrionic; his role as a priest is dignified.

The only way this problem can be solved is for that lifeless creature to become more sensitively aware of the physical and mental condition of his listeners. If he wants them to listen he can make them listen. He can quicken their senses, stimulate their imagination and focus their concentration on the most important thing in the life of the listening layman, his salvation. He can do it. I'm sure that this same lifeless body becomes very active when discussing some of the changes in the liturgy. Some of the most active conversations I have heard have been among priests discussing changes in the liturgy and the role of the laity. They're alive then because they're not thinking of maintaining an image. They're alive because they're thinking of convincing someone—changing someone's mind. Since it happens to be with other priests, they're safe. They don't have to worry about preserving an image. It's a human being talking to a human being with conviction and with strong intention to convince the listener.

The moment these same priests rise to the pulpit, they put on the public form which in many cases is the lifeless body.

Another sign which is really the opposite, but just as limiting, is the stiff, rigid body. This speaker understands that it is important to utilize all the energy, muster it all to the surface, because what is to be said is important. So he has developed the habit of excessive tension in his body, and what he doesn't realize is that he is strangling not only himself but his ideas. If you say to him, "Father, why don't you relax?", you know what he says? "Do you want me to be like the others? I've seen them. They're dead. I think you have to be alive!"

There's a third category: (they're really endless; they're as endless as the number of individual human beings who speak for Christ in the pulpit) signs and wonders in random activity. Random activity is identified by constant motion while speaking. What it really is, is the release of inner tension. But it appears—at least the speaker has convinced himself that it will appear—as complete freedom of the body and naturalness. Now this random activity, you should understand, is rather disconcerting to the eyes. If you find that your random activity helps to free your imagination and results in some flexibility of the voice, I wouldn't ask you to eliminate it. I would only ask you, before you begin to speak, to request your listeners to close their eyes and listen.

But my favorite body habit is apparently a tradition; it seems most priests are convinced that there is a particular physical appearance which must be assumed in order to maintain the image of the priest. The hands are slid up the sleeve and hidden there so as not to get in the way. Now if the layman who is watching were to reflect on what this reminds him of, he would probably tell you "a happy soul in a straightjacket." Why is it so many priests do this? Perhaps because they have seen hundreds of priests hide their hands up their sleeves; they conclude: it must be the right thing to do.

The fifth characteristic of body habits in oral communication reminds the listener, the looker really, of the 1900 elocutionary style. I'm sure you have seen, and a number of you will remember in your seminary life, a book in which you could find a diagram or sketch of what gesture you should use when trying to uplift hearts or what gesture you should use when you're trying to put the fear of God into someone's soul, and if you're against something, be sure that it's palms down.

Now this routine of rehearsing gestures in such a way that you have a finger meaning one thing and a position of a palm meaning another thing requires that we all have the same kind of bodies, that we all have the same kind of physical connection to psychic life—but we don't.

The system of trying to use precise gestures to mean precise things would ultimately require that you submit to your listeners in advance of your talk a dictionary of gestures: when my hand goes up that means . . ., and when my palms go down that means . . ., and when I hold my arms by my side—that's climax. This mechanical approach is no longer meaningful to the modern audience.

There is one last point in regard to the body, and that is the reverent, plaster face. Regardless of what has been said, whatever the words, whatever the theme, whatever the tongue, that face never changes. And the reason it never changes is probably because at some point (and it may have happened before ordination) someone said, "Don't ham it up." And if you don't ham it up no one can accuse you of being a phony. But if you cause that face to be out of tune with the workings of your mind and heart; if you speak of the love of Christ to other Christians, yet allow that face to be non-expressive, it's like pulling a shade down over a window. Because if the listener looks at this blank face he may, by a supreme act of concentration, somehow penetrate that wall and understand that the priest needs to talk to him, needs to share an idea that is vitally important to him. But a half hour or even ten minutes of this is going to be disconcerting. The listener is going to say either the poor man has muscular problems in his face or else he is not truly alive to that idea. He doesn't really believe in it! When you speak as Christ, you speak for the Tremendous Lover, and the life of that Love should be present in every part of your being. It does not mean that you have to be a Richard Burton vocally or a Cary Grant physically. It does mean that when another human being looks at you he will know you love. He will know regardless of how big or small, how fat or thin, how tall or short, or how ugly that mug. He will know that your soul's alive with love and reaching out to other human beings saying: "Let us love together."

Why do we allow these misconceptions and these bad habits to stop that love which we know is within us, which we constantly pray to increase within us? Why do we stop it? The body wasn't born that way. We made it lifeless. We made it stiff. We put it in a straight-jacket. We sent it to an elocutionary school and trained it to follow certain physical patterns and gestures. We keep that face immobile. It isn't natural. So what is the solution to this problem?

HUMAN NATURE

I ask you to begin with one thought. Consider the nature of the human being which you have spent years studying: the union of body and soul. Don't deny that union when you put that soul in act—in the act of communication. Allow that body freedom and recognize that that body has a natural right to live with the action of that soul when that soul is in direct communication with other souls. Remember that whatever is within your mind and heart that you are trying to inject in the mind and heart of the listener has to pass through his senses. Oral communication, like all knowledge, comes to and through the senses. Therefore, you have to check that what you are doing with your body and voice will awaken the senses of your listener to focus his mind on the material to be shared. In what positive way, then, is your body and voice contributing to that end communication, union?

PHYSICAL HABITS

Still, it isn't enough merely to understand the nature of communication; it is vitally important to prepare your body for communication, and you can't use age as an excuse. You can change your habits. You can change. But it requires determination, constant exercise and practice in which you constantly experiment with that body. So you have to exercise your body to participate in the life of your soul. You do it in all moments of heightened conversation. Your body is alive, at least to the extent that it is capable of being alive. You want it to become a vital part of the action of communication. You must allow the muscles of the body to feel with the thought in the mind. It is only in psychology and philosophy that we manage to dissect and departmentalize the soul: in fact, it is not departmentalized. In fact, it has a union with the body so that it lives with it in a single being. Consequently, if I have what I can identify as a purely intellectual idea then I must allow that body to live muscularly in a tone that is in keeping with the purely intellectual idea. I have talked with priests, and I have talked with congressmen and chairmen of national political parties; I am frequently told that the reason more isn't done with the voice and body is simply, "I am not making an emotional appeal." But when the mind is alive to an idea, and the being is directed towards the communication of that idea, the muscles of the body must be alive with it. Never, therefore, never allow your body to be literally passive when your mind is actively engaged in communication.

VOCAL HABITS

Those are a few of the observations about physical habits. There are many more very interesting habits vocally. Insufficient volume strikes the listener first. It is a simple thing. The layman sits in church and says, "I can't hear." He means simply "hear with my ears." Insufficient volume connects directly with the absence of physical vitality. That is, if the body is not alive, it is not likely that you are going to have sufficient volume. If there is no motor to get the vocal machinery moving then it is not likely the sound is going to carry.

One of the greatest dangers that accompanies advancing modern science and development in the presence of the microphone is lack of vocal energy. Someone warns not to blast the mike. That's true. Still, there is a way of controlling the voice, the volume of the voice, without killing the energy in the voice. It is possible to speak higher, quietly, but energetically. Now what happens to many speakers the minute they get a microphone is they speak quietly at the expense of energy. Lack of energy in the voice is the second element or characteristic which identifies the poor oral communicator.

On the other hand, it is possible for a speaker to have volume without energy. You hear it frequently. It is a hollow sound. It is a cymbal sound. It is the sound of the empty barrel. It is loud but it is empty. It is possible to have volume without having energy. What do you do about that? Be concerned with being heard, with being understood, and with touching something beyond the ear of the listener and you will probably have sufficient volume and sufficient energy because it isn't just physical energy we are talking about here. It is spiritual, intellectual energy in the moment of communication that connects with that body and voice. And if that isn't present, if that intellectual energy is not there, and the spiritual energy is not there, and the need to touch those other human beings is not there, you may use all the volume that you like and you will still be empty.

We human beings are very skilled in one thing. At least we all practice it whether we are skilled in it or not. And that is seeing through each other. The moment I stand up, you make a judgment. The moment I open my mouth, you make a judgment. Now I protest: you are wrong! But I can't stop you from making a judgment. The congregation, those laymen who sit there, make judgments. And they look for the signs to convince themselves that you are not really interested in them, that you don't really care, that you don't truly understand. They can tell by the vague look in the eye. They can tell by the dead sound of the voice. They can tell by the abstractness of the language. We look and listen on the surface at the manner of the body and to the sound of words and in the eye of the communicator. We look and listen and we make judgments on the basis of what we see and hear.

Open up all of yourself. Don't hide any of yourself out of fear that someone will find out how frightened you are or how ignorant you are. Don't pull back. The moment you try to protect the self, you hide that part of yourself which is most powerful as an instrument for love. Love has to move out and towards. You cannot proceed to love by protecting self. And since the act of communicating the Word of God is a specific act of love, you cannot protect yourself. You cannot worry about what any one person may think. You are loving.

Now, there is a vocal quality with which I know you are all familiar. It is the monotone— the vocal quality that lacks flexibility.
It results from a failure to realize that the voice should move with the
idea. The voice is the piano. The mind is the player. And if the
ideas in that mind are specific pieces of music, you must play on that
instrument so that someone else can hear the melody, not just the
sound. The voice is an instrument as the body is an instrument, and
it should be free enough and flexible enough to be at the service of
the ideas in the mind—the music to be played.

Often, in place of flexibility, pauses are used for emphasis—pauses
through which you could drive trucks. A pause is valid only if it
intensifies the idea that has just been expressed or builds some kind
of suspense on what is about to be expressed. A pause should not be
used as a resting place for the speaker. It should not be used by the
speaker to convince the listener that in case he has not yet gotten the
idea he is hearing very significant thoughts. You get the feeling when
you hear this kind of talk with lots of pauses that this is assurance,
that this man knows what he is doing. He is confident; he is not nervous. He is not communicating but he is not nervous! You must not be
afraid variety and flexibility will turn you into a ham. It takes years
of work to be a ham. But the voice should always be at the command
of the idea and the significance of the idea. The voice should be made
to move, up or down, loud or soft, fast or slow. And the basis of
whether or not that idea needs vocal adjustment and change is effective communication.

The preachy tone is another block to communication. And the
preachy tone is a combination of factors. It has variety. It has
flexibility. It also has within it that sound of condescension—that
"we are gathered here today" tone—that the listener identifies as from
another world. And it is indeed from another world. It is not from
the world of this soul speaking. It is from some developed habit, a
habit that doesn't connect with the senses, the needs, the interest of
the human beings listening, or the human being speaking. It can have
the sound of proficiency; it can have the sound of professionalism.
But if it doesn't have the sound of a human being, if it has the sound
of a preacher, it is not the sound of a person.

A number of people say that you must not speak too quickly. Set
that up as a principle, and the result is a measured, monotonous
tempo. By this measured tempo of speaking—supposedly designed to
assist the listener in understanding clearly the words that are being
spoken—I am talking now about another element of communication
which has nothing to do with communion among human beings. It
has nothing to do with having a conversation with someone. It has
everything to do with a phony notion of how tempo comes into play
in communication. This tempo is the tempo of a man who believes

that it is necessary to speak clearly and slowly when the fact again is that that voice should move in relation to the capacity of the listener to understand. If you can comprehend 500 words a minute, then I should speak 500 words a minute. The rate at which I speak should be adjusted by the rate you need to comprehend the meaning of the words I speak.

Finally, slovenly speech often comes out of the American concept of the average man. Don't speak too clearly. If you do, you're a phony. Let the sounds kind of merge with each other so that you will have a natural effect on people. But, if they don't grasp the symbols, if they don't hear those sounds clearly, it is impossible for them to think about what you are saying. It is possible for them to think about you and your needs or to think about themselves and their own needs, but they will not be thinking about what you are saying. It is not natural to misuse an instrument. And although speech is an overlaid function, it is nevertheless obviously intended as a means of contact. Thus, there is nothing wrong with shaping the words clearly.

On the other hand there is something wrong with using an occasion of communication as an exercise for your articulators. If you use an excessive amount of lip movement thinking that you are forming the sounds with your lips only, it is very distracting because the listener is saying, "Look at all that action." He sees that action in the face which is more interesting than the action in the mind. It is not necessary to overdo to be heard. The tongue is the principle articulator, the mouth must be opened, of course, to allow the sound to go forward, the lips must not be lazy, but excessive movement of the lips is very distracting to watch. Still, in private practice I would recommend that you overarticulate in order to get those muscles active, particularly if you have been, for a number of years, a mumbler—but not in public.

EAR TRAINING

To solve these problems you must first train your ear. You have to hear it, to be able to identify it. You can train your ear not only by listening to yourself on a tape recorder, but also by listening to professional speakers. Try to hear why they are good. What elements in their voice, what elements in their quality of speech make it interesting to listen to, make it clear, vital and varied. And don't hesitate to imitate. As long as you're imitating the best, you are on the right track for personal development.

I am not saying imitate them in public. Don't ever use an occasion of communication as a moment of exercise. Never practice on people when they think that you are engaged in an act of love for them. A moment of communication is an opportunity to establish some kind of significant union, some kind of significant contact with other human beings. It is not an exercise period.

Still, you have to exercise if you intend to develop better and more effective habits. It is a foolish waste of time to worry about how good you are as a speaker without doing something about improving yourself. The only way to improve, however, is to practice, exercising for volume control, tone control, tempo control and variation, variety of pitch, clarity of speech—one element at a time.

MEANING INTO SOUND

The objective ultimately here in working on your voice and your habit of speech is to find a way to put the meaning into a sound—to put the meaning of what you are saying in the sound of your voice. From the time we began school we were taught how to write while we weren't required to consider how we communicate vocally, despite the fact that we spend most of our lives talking, not writing. Talking we were told is natural, but writing is a *skill,* and you have to learn how to write. To speak well, however, just be your natural self. As a result, the odds are that you can write far more effectively than you can *speak,* despite the years of experience in speaking.

It is a writer's habit, whether he is a highly skilled creative writer or just a letter writer, to believe that once he has put his thought on paper, the idea is there *now* because he wrote it. His assumption is that because he put the verbal symbols on the paper, communication has taken place. So a speaker who has finished writing his speech believes that the idea exists on the paper, forgetting that it is only a series of symbols. The moment he stands before the lectern with the paper in front of him, his habit frequently is to rely on *reporting* the words that are on the printed page without allowing the meaning of those words to be *recreated* within him mentally and spiritually. What the speaker felt, the moment he captured and selected those words in the writing, must be recreated in the speaking of them or they die. That's really what interpretation is.

We make the mistake of believing, "I have it here. I spent hours on it. I am sure if you don't understand what I am saying you will understand it if you read the cards." That's not true. The speaker cannot rely on the printed words before him. He has to try to make these words go back to the idea which caused them. The inclination is, "I like the way I said this," and now he is talking about it as if it is somebody else's thing, and we are all looking at it—instead of allowing that idea to come to life within him. If you cannot recreate the idea and the feeling which accompanied the idea at the time you wrote the homily, I say: mimeograph it and distribute the copies. The odds are that you will communicate that idea much more effectively that way because you spent more time putting the idea down on paper than you spent concerning yourself with how to translate those verbal symbols into vocal sounds.

Those are some of the misconceptions which constitute obstacles to the full use of self in communication. Those are a few of the habits which the layman identifies in the use of the body and voice in communication.

NEED TO COMMUNICATE

Here is a final thought: You must train your mind as well as your bodies and voices to realize that your idiosyncracies—your shyness, your natural reticence, your apprehension about making a fool of yourself, and your theories about effective communication—all must be suppressed, erased, replaced. In other words, in a sense, you don't count! At least all those negatives don't count—all those things *you don't want to be* aren't important. What *you must be* is vitally important. You must be subject to the needs, and filled with zeal in meeting the needs, of communicating the Word. Your interest here indicates that we can assume that you are determined to meet the demands of communicating effectively the Word of God—communicating the Word of God in a world of sophisticated listeners.

So what are you going to do? First of all, remember that it takes time to change. To improve the habits of the voice and body and the speech means to change. You cannot improve without change. Everyone wants to improve. It is very hard to find people who want to change. And changing habits always, or nearly always, involves a feeling of phoniness, or awkwardness, because it does take time to cultivate new habits—but *experiment*. And if you experiment with your imagination, your body, and your voice, don't mince around with minor little changes of a finger gesture here, or a pitch change there—really experiment! Take some giant steps. And don't predict the outcome. Try anything at least *twice*. Remember it isn't going to be easy to change those natural habits of immobility, monotone, and indistinctiveness.

The Word of God does indeed need the natural, but not the subconscious efforts we make to *seem* natural, to *seem* humble, and to *seem* average. The Word of God needs, and has the right to, the fullest use of our individual natures, our minds and hearts, our bodies and our voices. The extraordinary Word of God must be communicated through the extraordinary use of self. Now certainly we rely on the Holy Spirit and we must, but it is reasonable to assume that the Holy Spirit would welcome a little more assistance from us. And because of the words of St. Paul, "Woe to me if I preach not the Gospel," you know far better than I do how vital it is, how vital is your need to develop more fully your ability to communicate the rich-ness, the spiritual richness of Catholicism in a way that will stimulate recognition of its significance for contemporary living.

The development of this ability will require, in fact it demands, much effort, energy, sweat, tediousness, and annoyance. It helps sometimes to remember where we stand when we do less than our best, when we give less than our most—we're lukewarm. As com-municators we all become lukewarm at times because we begin to think the listener doesn't care.

After 15 years of teaching it's so easy to think this that I sit in my room saying, "Why am I wasting all this energy? They don't care. I am dropping these pearls of wisdom and they are not really inter-ested. They don't understand the value of what I am saying to them." And I am tempted to coast. Yet when I begin to coast as an educator or as a communicator then I begin to become lukewarm.

You can't give up. Laymen want to hear. They really want to feel. They really want to love. But like all lovers, except the Tre-mendous Lover, we need a push, we need a stimulant, we need redi-rection. And that means that somebody has to become active first— that's you! You love, and they will love back.

Each one of you has experienced a layman saying to you (but not frequently enough), "Father, I didn't get it. I don't know what you were getting at." You would welcome this, I think. You would also welcome someone saying, "Father, thanks, I needed that." You have to encourage laymen to speak up. And you have to *mean* it when you say, "Tell me what you think," because when they say, "Father, I didn't get it," you shouldn't say: "Well, what do you mean you didn't get it? I made it perfectly clear."

Communication must begin between the priest and the layman and it can't be limited to a 10-minute part of the Mass. It can't be only 10 minutes a week. It has to be a communication of the spirit. It has to be a recognition that we are not so far apart. The divisions which are constantly analyzed in various forward-looking publica-tions about the clergy over there and the laymen over here must be eliminated. Valueless distinctions are being made between the role of the laity and the role of the clergy. What unites us in a com-munion of the Mystical Body of Christ is far more important than what identifies our roles in the institution of the Church. We are both trying to work out salvation. I am looking to you for guidance—I, the layman; I need your inspiration and your knowledge; I don't need perfection from you in sound; I don't need perfection in literary style, although perfection in form and style will facilitate my response, per-haps. But the important thing I need is the feeling that someone is alive and loving me together in Christ. And if I get that feeling instead of the feeling of another instruction, another explanation instead of an act of love, I cannot continue in my complacency. I cannot continue to point the finger of accusation towards the institution of the Church and towards the deficiencies and complacency of the members of the clergy. For once I see someone alive with love, no one in the world can deny it, even those who denied Christ. Even those who deny the "Tremendous Lover" must respond positively. And the worst thing that is happening in the Church is this—there is no response.

Last Sunday as I stood at the gospel, I couldn't understand what the priest was reading. Since I was in the wing of the church, I looked at the 400 faces in the congregation and I didn't see one face that suggested to me that it was hearing the Word of God proclaimed—not one!

Is it a ritual only? "Now we read the epistle, now we read the gospel. Now we have a little homily. Then we go back to the Mass." It can't be that way because any break that takes place in the act of love which is the Holy Sacrifice of the Mass is wrong. The homily has to be a continuation of that perfect act of love, the Holy Sacrifice of the Mass. It has to sustain what has been begun. It must be a bridge in the structure of the liturgy from the service of the Word to the service of the Bread.

You can even speak in double negatives. You can speak in a nasal twang. You can speak with your hands in your ears! But if you are in love with what you are saying and with the people with whom you are saying it, then those words of yours will be a vital part of that sacrifice.

With a selfless approach, to use the self fully, with a considerable amount of sweat to develop new and more effective habits, and with the aid of the Holy Spirit always, you can be more perfect instruments through which the Word may be heard, the hearts of the faithful filled, and the fire of His love enkindled in us all.

THE THEOLOGY OF PREACHING

by

Reverend Richard Hanley, O.M.I.

INTRODUCTION

One of the most refreshing theological trends of the twentieth century has been the emphasis placed on the "ministry of the word" (Acts 6:4). As with so many other theological studies, it has been like the discovery of an old diamond that has always existed in the Church's doctrinal treasure-chest, but which has been made to shine resplendently by the polishing of recent theological investigation. Various factors have provided impetus to contemporary theological endeavors aimed at better understanding and appreciating the ministry of the word. Among the outstanding influences are five specific factors indicated by Fathers Alszeghy, S.J., and Flick, S.J., in an excellent article on which they collaborated entitled: "The Theological Problem of Preaching." [1]

Theoretical analyses of preaching have first of all been conceived by exigencies deriving from the practical order. Contemporary preaching praxis has oftentimes occasioned widespread dissatisfaction both on the part of priests engaged in pastoral work as well as on the part of an increasingly better educated laity. Such a situation serves to confirm the wisdom of Father Jungmann's adage: "In questions of great importance, nothing is more practical than a good theory." [2]

A second contributing element has been the current philosophical emphasis dealing with the theory of values. This healthy speculation has given rise to questions concerning motivation in Christian life, has been applied in modern catechetical pedagogy, and has exerted a favorable influence on the technique of modern preaching.

17

The demands of the pastoral ministry and the stimulating thought of philosophy, however, could never produce a true theology of preaching unless a profound study of the sources had already provided us with abundant material for theological reflection. This third factor has been fostered above all by the tremendous strides of modern Biblical scholarship. Research in patristic studies has also helped immensely, as well as some positive works on the great theologians of the Middle Ages.

A fourth element of major import has been the liturgical movement. The encyclical *Mediator Dei* included the homily in the totality of the Church's "liturgical action," [3] and the Second Vatican Council has declared the sermon to be "part of the liturgical service"; [4] and again: "the homily . . . is to be highly esteemed as part of the liturgy itself." [5] Also, a deeper realization of the intimate union between the sacraments and preaching has been one of the most noble births of contemporary liturgical studies.

It is common knowledge that since the sixteenth century Protestant emphasis on preaching has never been lacking. Their efforts have stimulated Catholic scholars to extensive research into this hitherto neglected area of Catholic theology.

The ecumenical spirit of the present day is adding vital impetus to this study, and not a few scholars have expressed the feeling that the road to union is more hopeful in that the Church today is stressing the importance of the ministry of the word, and the separated brethren are emphasizing the necessity of the sacraments. [6]

Finally, the impetus of the Second Vatican Council has had a tremendous impact on the ministry of the word. The pastoral concern of the Council to make the gospel message relevant to the people of today will be fulfilled to a great extent only by meaningful preaching of the word of God.

Although one will search in vain for a detailed treatise on the theology of preaching in our classic systematic theology, nevertheless the present posing of the problem is not an entirely new entity. Many notions necessary for such a potential treatise have already been elaborated in other tracts. However, anyone with eyes to see is aware of the growing number of specific works in recent years dealing with the Bible and preaching, the liturgy and preaching, theology and preaching, etc. The term "theology of preaching" simply means theological reflection on the meaning of the ministry of the word.

The term "preaching" as contained in the title of this paper is to be understood in the sense of the exercise of the sacred ministry entrusted to the apostles and their successors by our Lord Jesus Christ when He commissioned them to "go into the whole world and preach the gospel to every creature" (Mk 16:15). This is equivalent to the exercise of what our present Code of Canon Law calls *praedicatio verbi divini* in can. 1327-1328, and more specifically *concio sacra* in can. 1337-1348.

The term 'praedicatio' can be understood in a twofold sense: first, as something that is said before, that is, prior to that event, and thus it implies a prophecy; secondly, as something that is said before, this is, in the presence of someone, and thus it implies an exhortation. It is in the latter meaning that the term is to be understood. The word 'preach' has come into the English language from the Latin through the French. The term 'concio' in the early Latin meant a meeting place or a convention. In the course of the centuries it came to mean the discourse held at or during a meeting. Hence today this word designates the sermon.[7]

More precisely, preaching may be defined as "the public proposal of the word of God in the name of the Church." [8]

THE DIGNITY OF THE OFFICE OF PREACHING

In the only papal encyclical dealing exclusively with preaching the word of God, Benedict XV declared:

It was the desire of Jesus Christ, once He had wrought the redemption of the human race by His death on the altar of the cross, to lead men to obey His commands and thus win eternal life. To attain this end He used no other means than the voice of His heralds whose work it was to announce to all mankind what they had to believe and to do in order to be saved. "It pleased God, by the foolishness of our preaching, to save those who believe" (I Cor 1:21). He chose therefore His apostles and after infusing into their minds by the power of the Holy Spirit the gifts in harmony with their high calling, "go into the whole world," He told them, "and preach the Gospel" (Mk 16:15). Their preaching renewed the face of the earth. For if the religion of Christ has withdrawn the minds of men from errors of every kind to the truth and won their hearts from the degradation of vice to the excellence and beauty of every virtue, assuredly it has done so by that very preaching. "Faith depends on hearing, and hearing on the word of Christ" (Rom 10:17). Wherefore since by God's good pleasure, things are preserved through the same causes by which they were brought into being, it is evident that the preaching of the wisdom taught by the Christian religion is the means divinely employed to continue the work of eternal salvation, and that it must with just reason be looked upon as a matter of greatest and most momentous concern.[9]

Here, in a nutshell, is a whole theology of preaching. The Holy Father describes preaching as the principal divinely constituted means for prolonging the salvific mission of Christ in the world, for proposing to men the way of salvation, and for the propagation and building up of the kingdom of God. The bishop's admonition to priests on their ordination day quite naturally comes to mind here: "by your preaching . . . may you build the house that is the family of God." [10]

Preaching is not essential to religion as such, indeed it is absent from many of the world's great religions, the exceptions being Judaism, Christianity and Buddhism.[11] The essentialness of preaching, to Christianity, is wholly dependent upon the will of its Founder. Because Christ willed preaching to be an ordinary means of salvation, it not only exists, but must exist; it cannot be discarded.

The Savior's will is manifest from his own words and works and from the historical intellection of his words by the apostles and the Church. Our Lord himself expressly stated that the purpose of his mission on earth was to preach the good news of salvation to mankind: "Let us go into the neighboring villages and towns, that there also I may preach. For this is why I have come. And he was preaching in their synagogues, and throughout all Galilee, and casting out devils" (Mk 1:38-39). Or as Luke puts it: "To the other towns also I must proclaim the kingdom of God, for this is why I have been sent. And he was preaching in the synagogues of Galilee" (Lk 4:43-44). Again: "And he came to Nazareth, where he had been brought up; and according to his custom, he entered the synagogue on the Sabbath and stood up to read. And the volume of Isaias the prophet was handed to him. And after he opened the volume, he found the place where it was written, the Spirit of the Lord is upon me because he has anointed me; to bring good news to the poor he has sent me, to proclaim to the captives release, and sight to the blind; to set at liberty the oppressed, to proclaim the acceptable year of the Lord, and the day of recompense. And closing the volume, he gave it back to the attendant and sat down. And the eyes of all in the synagogue were gazing on him. But he began to say to them, today this Scripture has been fulfilled in your hearing. And all bore witness and marvelled at the words of grace that came from his mouth" (Lk 4:16-22). The characteristics of the promised Messiah enumerated by Isaias the prophet are fulfilled in Christ and first and foremost of these is "to bring good news to the poor" (Lk 4:18), salvation. As Mark put it so succinctly: "And after John had been delivered up, Jesus came into Galilee, preaching the gospel of the kingdom of God, and saying, the time is fulfilled, and the kingdom of God is at hand. Repent and believe in the gospel" (Mk 1:14-15).

The Second Vatican Council has explicitly stated that preaching was the ordinary means of salvation used by Christ:

> The mystery of the holy Church is manifested in its very foundation. The Lord Jesus set it on its course by preaching the good news, that is, the coming of the kingdom of God, which, for centuries, had been promised in the Scriptures; 'The time is fulfilled, and the kingdom of God is at hand' (Mk 1:15). In the word, in the works, and in the presence of Christ, this kingdom was clearly open to the view of men. The word of the Lord is compared to a

seed which is sown in a field (Mk 4:14); those who hear the word with faith and become part of the little flock of Christ (Lk 12:30), have received the kingdom itself.[12]

Christ sends his apostles on a temporary mission during his public life, commanding them: "And as you go, preach the message, the kingdom of heaven is at hand! Cure the sick, raise the dead, cleanse the lepers, cast out devils. Freely you have received, freely give" (Mk 10:7-8). The twelve will heal the sick, raise the dead, cleanse lepers and cast out devils, but preaching salvation is their primary mandate.

And in his last will and testament to them, just before ascending to his Father, Jesus commissioned them: "Go into the whole world and preach the gospel to every creature. He who believes and is baptized shall be saved, but he who does not believe shall be condemned" (Mk 16:15-16).

The apostles clearly understood and obeyed the Master's command, for Mark continues: "They went forth and preached everywhere, while the Lord worked with them and confirmed the preaching by the signs that followed" (Mk 16:20). On Pentecost, the apostles "were all filled with the Holy Spirit" (Acts 2:4) and spoke to the multitudes "of the wonderful works of God" (Acts 2:11). Peter publicly announced the kerygma of the Savior who had suffered, died, risen, and lives on to vivify with divine life all who believe in him.[13] "Now they who received his word were baptized, and there were added that day about three thousand souls" (Acts 2:41).

From that time on, the apostles ceased not to preach Christ who had come "to give his life as a ransom for many" (Mk 1:45), for salvation is to be found only in him.[14] Every dawn became a new occasion to proclaim the "Son of Justice", the "Light of the World", and the "Day of the Lord:" every place became a pulpit to announce Jesus, be it the temple, the synagogues, the courts of rulers, private homes, or the street corners of cities; every audience became a potential "people of God," be it Galileans or Judeans, Parthians or Medes, Elamites or Mesopotamians, Cappadocians or Egyptians,[15] thousands of persons or only a handful. The apostles had only one concern, to make Christ known: "we cannot but speak of what we have seen and heard" (Acts 4:20). They preferred preaching to everything else, even to things dear to their hearts as "other Christs." When charitable works jeopardized the precious time needed for preaching, they delegated this noble work to others: "It is not desirable that we should forsake the word of God and serve at tables . . . we will devote ourselves to prayer and to the ministry of the word" (Acts 6:2-4). Just as Christ had delegated the administration of baptism to his disciples,[16] so too Paul did the same and justified his procedure by appealing to the mission he had received: "Christ did not send me to baptize, but to preach the gospel" (I Cor 1:17).

When Peter and John were charged by the Sanhedrin "not to speak or to teach at all in the name of Jesus, . . . they answered and said to them, 'Whether it is right in the sight of God to listen to you rather than to God, decide for yourselves. For we cannot but speak of what we have seen and heard' " (Acts 4:18-20). Again, when Peter and the apostles were imprisoned for preaching Christ, "during the night an angel of the Lord opened the doors of the prison and let them out, and said, 'Go stand and speak in the temple to the people all the words of this life' " (Acts 5:19-20). And having been scourged and warned anew not to preach Christ, "they departed from the presence of the Sanhedrin, rejoicing that they had been counted worthy to suffer disgrace for the name of Jesus. And they did not for a single day cease teaching and preaching in the temple and from house to house the good news of Jesus as the Christ" (Acts 5:40-42).

Aware of the nearness of persecution and death, Paul's conscience was at peace since he had always been faithful to the ministry "received from the Lord Jesus" (Acts 20:24), and he knew that the Lord always stood by him and strengthened him in his preaching of the gospel.[17] His last will and testament to Timothy was a Pauline echo of Christ's final mandate to his apostles: "Preach the word, be urgent in season, out of season; reprove, entreat, rebuke . . . work as a preacher of the gospel, fulfill thy ministry" (II Tim 4:2, 5). Commenting on these words, Father Spicq applied them to all priests:

> These are the last words Saint Paul wrote, the last order he prescribed, and they sum up all the precepts and counsels he gave to Timothy. The apostle's testament, his last will, is to exhort his disciple to devote himself to preaching. The tenses of the verbs and the context imply that this office is to continue until the end of time. Saint Paul assumed its obligations during his lifetime; his successors will have to continue his work after his departure. The priest, according to Saint Paul, has for his essential role the preaching of the word of God, instructing the faithful.[18]

With the death of the apostles, their successors through the ages have ever been mindful of their heritage to preach the gospel. Trent taught that preaching is "the principal function of bishops." [19] The Fathers of the Second Vatican Council, whose chief pastoral concern is towards the accomplishment of the universal task of evangelization and salvation entrusted by Christ to his Church, solemnly declared:

> As the Son was sent by the Father (Jn 20:21), so He too sent the apostles, saying: "Go, therefore, and make disciples of all nations, baptizing them in the name of the Father, and of the Son, and of the Holy Spirit, teaching them to observe all that I have commanded you; and behold, I am with you all days, even unto the consummation of the world" (Mt 28:18-20). The Church has received this solemn mandate of Christ to proclaim the saving truth from the apostles and must carry it out to the very ends of the earth (Acts 1:8). Wherefore she makes the

words of the Apostle her own: "Woe to me if I do not preach the gospel" (I Cor 9:16), and continues unceasingly to send heralds of the gospel until such time as the infant churches are fully established and can themselves continue the work of evangelizing. For the Church is compelled by the Holy Spirit to do her part that God's plan may be fully realized, whereby He has constituted Christ as the source of salvation for the whole world. By the proclamation of the gospel she prepares her hearers to receive and profess the faith. She gives them the dispositions necessary for baptism, snatches them from the slavery of error and of idols and incorporates them in Christ so that through charity they may grow up into full maturity in Christ.[20]

Pope John XXIII taught that preaching is "the principal work and the high point of the Catholic priesthood, and for the bishops in particular," [21] but that all priests, precisely because they are priests, are called to the direct pastoral ministry of souls.[22] Although only those with the care of souls are obliged in justice to preach, namely pastors, quasi-pastors and parochial vicars who are endowed with the full parochial power,[23] nevertheless, the nature of the priesthood is the same in all priests, and therefore all are ordained to preach as well as sacrifice.

A priest who knew well how to celebrate the holy sacrifice, the 'Breaking of Bread,' but did not know how to break the bread of the word of God to the faithful, would be only half a priest.[24]

Priests will be called upon by God to render an account not merely for themselves but for the salvation of the whole world.[25] As the Second Vatican Council teaches:

Priests, although they do not possess the highest degree of the priesthood, and although they are dependent on the bishops in the exercise of their power, nevertheless, they are united with the bishops in sacerdotal dignity. By the power of the sacrament of Order, in the image of Christ the eternal high priest (Heb 5:1-10), they are consecrated to preach the gospel and shepherd the faithful and to celebrate divine worship, so that they are true priests of the New Testament. Partakers of the function of Christ the sole Mediator (I Tim 2:5), on their level of ministry, they announce the divine word to all.[26]

Finally, Paul VI, in his first encyclical letter, spoke of the "supreme importance" of preaching in these words:

No other form of communication can take its place; not even the enormously powerful technical means of press, radio and television. In a sense, the apostlate and preaching are the same. Preaching is the primary apostolate. Our apostolate, Venerable Brothers, is above all the ministry of the word. We know this very well, but it seems good to remind ourselves of it now, so as to direct our pastoral activities aright.[27]

Ten years previous, as Monsignor Montini, he had said: "There is no task more essential then to proclaim the word of God, no labor more apostolic than to carry out . . . the mission of preaching the gospel."[28]

Therefore, the essentialness, importance, and necessity of preaching the gospel is deeply rooted in the will of Christ, who bequeathed the ministry of the word to his Church as the primary means of accomplishing its universal mission of salvation.[29] The excellence and dignity of preaching, therefore, lies in the fact that it is the divinely chosen human means through which God speaks to men,[30] and is therefore an essential element in the structure of the Church revealed by Christ. As the Second Vatican Council put it in the Constitution on the Liturgy: "God wills that all men be saved and come to the knowledge of the truth (I Tim 2:4), who in many and various ways spoke in times past to the prophets" (Heb 1:1), when the fullness of time had come sent his Son, the Word made flesh, anointed by the Holy Spirit, to preach the gospel to the poor. . . ." [31]

But is it possible to possess an insight into the "why" of this divine decree? It would certainly seem so. Christianity is the religion of the Incarnation, of the revelation of the fullness of divine truth to mankind in Christ: "I have come into the world to bear witness to the truth" (Jn 18:37). This truth, however, is pregnant with divine mystery, and as such does not force the mind of man into submission, but rather includes a strong appeal to man's liberty to surrender himself freely to the truth in faith.[32] But "faith depends on hearing, and hearing on the word of Christ" (Rom 10:17), the divine Word in person, whose words re-echo through the voices of his duly appointed preachers, and whoever believes them will be saved.[33] The initial proposal of divine truth was made by Christ, the Word in person, and since His Ascension and until His Parousia, through the words of His preachers, who have "gone forth and preached everywhere" (Mk 16:20), so that their sound has gone forth into all the world and their words resound unto the ends of the earth.[34] In the time of our Lord, therefore, the free acceptance or rejection of His person included the acceptance or rejection of his doctrine; since His Ascension, the assent to or rejection of his doctrine implies an acceptance or renouncement of his person, of the Word, who is the fullness of truth: "I am the . . . Truth" (Jn 14:5). In God's revelation to man, as Father Spicq has so aptly noted, salvation is synonymous with knowledge of the truth. "God," writes St. Paul, "wishes all men to be saved and to come to the knowledge of the truth" (I Tim 2:4).[35] Our Blessed Lord said that eternal life will be given to whoever will have known the true God and the only Son sent by God (Jn 17:3). It should be pointed out too that "truth" in the Bible very often designates the rectitude of one's moral life in accord with the divine will. Father Braun has shown how this is especially true of Saint John, for whom those who believe and love "are of the truth" (I Jn 3:19).[36] The will of Christ, therefore, is ultimately responsible for the vicarious role that preaching plays in salvation history, but it is a will which is understandable to us by reason of the very nature of our Savior's message: divine truth, freely proposed, that can be freely embraced in a spirit of faith or freely rejected. Thus it is clear why Benedict XV would say:

> The high dignity of the ministry entrusted to preachers comes from the fact that it is the continuation of the work of Jesus Christ. The divine Savior stated clearly to the Apostles and through them to all His future ministers; "as the Father has sent me, I also send you" (Jn 20:21). Then, in order to show how they were to continue His mission, Jesus Christ, who on another occasion had said that He had "come into the world to bear witness to the truth" (Jn 18:37), added the command: "Preach the Gospel" (Mk 16:15). One can easily understand, therefore, how Christ Who could say of Himself in the strictest sense of the expression: "I am the light of the world" (Jn 8:12), could also, in His infinite goodness, describe as "the light of the world" those who, in union with Him and through Him, were destined to spread the light of truth throughout the world: "You are the light of the world" (Mt 5:14).[37]

The very first words of the Second Vatican Council's *Constitution on the Church* speak in a similar vein: "Christ is the light of nations. Because this is so, this Sacred Synod gathered together in the Holy Spirit eagerly desires, by proclaiming the gospel to every creature (Mk 16:15), to bring the light of Christ to all men." [38]

The importance of preaching in the present economy of salvation, therefore, can hardly be overstressed, and one can readily understand Benedict XV's paternal admonition to his priests:

> Value highly your exalted vocation, beloved sons, you who have embraced the ministry of sacred preaching, for it is by means of this that you have been made continuators of God's work.[39]

Indeed, preaching is so intimately bound to the Church's life that in salvation history the "time of the Church" is the "time of preaching." [40] The present age is one of tension between the "already" and the "not yet." The Savior has come into history and he will come again in majesty. In the meantime he comes in mystery through the life of faith communicated by the light of the gospel proclaimed by his heralds. If the criterion at the final judgment is to be man's attitude vis-a-vis the gospel (II Thess 1:7-10), then all men must be given an opportunity to hear the word of God. And how are they to hear if no one preaches (Rom 10:14)? This is why Saint Paul felt personally obliged to labor unceasingly in the preaching of the gospel, for his activity was a factor on which God had made the definitive coming of his kingdom dependent.[41] The fulfillment of this divine mandate is so essential to the life of the Church that some authors consider it to be a negative note of the Church.[42] In this sense: if preaching ceased to pulse in the Church's organism, it would no more be the true Church of Jesus Christ than a church with only six sacraments. Surely there is no question here of the cessation of preaching by mere external force, as in persecuted countries, but rather of the exclusion of preaching from the very constitutive structure of the Church. Our Lord brought salvation to the world and used only one principal means to convey his religious message to men. the ministry of the word. "The religion which claims him as its author must be a religion of the Word." [43]

PURPOSE OF PREACHING

Although there is an infinite distance between the work accomplished by Christ and that of his preachers, who prolong his salvific mission of proposing to mankind the way of salvation, nevertheless, the goal or purpose of both is essentially the same. The character of any work is ennobled the more it approaches the end intended by God, the *"Alpha* and the *Omega"* (Apoc 1:8) of all things. The excellence of preaching consists precisely in the fact that it is beyond any category of "nearness" to the divine intent, for it belongs to the realm of "identity" with the divine purpose.[44]

Like all of man's conscious activity, preaching is ultimately intended to promote the glory of God, but it actually accomplishes this in so far as it effects the salvation of men. How are men "saved?" By coming into living contact with the objective redemption accomplished by the risen Christ. There are two possible paths that lead man to this vital insertion into Christ's life—faith and baptism: "He who believes and is baptized shall be saved" (Mk 16:16).[45] Our Lord, however, prefaced these words with a command that explains how faith and baptism would be made known to men: "Go into the whole world and preach the gospel" (Mk 16:15). Even in infant baptism the child is incorporated into Christ through an act of faith made in its name by the godparents or by the Church, the community of believers.[46] The first question proposed to the recipient of this "sacrament of faith" [47] is: "What do you ask of the Church of God?" and the reply: "The faith." The second question is: "What does the faith offer you," and the reply: "Eternal life." [48] Baptism, therefore, and the other sacraments too, bring man into living contact with Christ's redemptive salvation. Saint Thomas has noted well, however, that the sacraments are also "signs which proclaim the faith by which a man is justified," [49] and the Second Vatican Council's *Constitution on the Liturgy* has reiterated the same doctrine,[50] but this faith must first be proposed to a man before he can believe explicitly, and in the case of someone baptized as an infant, proposed to him in adulthood in order that he might ratify the act of faith made previously in his stead by his godparents. "Without faith it is impossible to please God" (Heb 11:6), for faith is the beginning, foundation and source of all justification.[51]

In the course of history, God has spoken directly to very few people, preferring to speak indirectly through the medium of his appointed heralds, who, for the most part, have also heard him only mediately themselves. Since the coming of Christ into the world, the preaching of the Church has been the ordinary divine organ for proclaiming the faith to mankind. The Church's mission is related to the Incarnation in so far as it prolongs the mission of the Word made flesh. Both missions are finalized by the same goal—the salvation of men. But the union is more profound than that effected by mere finality, for the end is achieved by the same principle of life which Christ possesses within himself and communicates to the ministers by the power of his Spirit.[52] Preaching purposes therefore to propose the object and motive of faith to mankind. In conjunction with God's grace, which draws the hearer to assent by illuminating his mind and moving his will, preaching functions to engender faith[53] by which the hearer is made to share in salvation.[54] "It pleased God, by the foolishness of our preaching, to save those who believe" (I Cor 1:21).

The purpose of preaching is not merely to impart knowledge as such, but rather to effect a vital, personal, faith-filled commitment to Christ who is encountered in the hearing of the word of God. As Father Cordovani has said so well: "Preaching . . . is ordained essentially to faith and salvation. . . . Faith blossoms forth in love, but it is born by hearing God's word."[55] In aiming at this goal of conversion or of growth in faith, the preacher, like Christ Himself, appeals to his hearer's intellect, will and emotions—in a word, to the whole man. The believer's response will include an enrichment of hope and an enkindling of charity as well as a growth in faith, all of which will make him a more faithful Christian, full of faith in the living Christ who dwells in his soul—"He who is just lives by faith" (Rom 1:17).

This broad notion of man's faith-reply to the revealing God's salutation through the medium of his commissioned preacher is thoroughly Biblical.[56] The believer does not give a mere intellectual assent to revealed truth, for it is a human act which engages his total personality and affects his whole attitude toward life. The analogy with the consumption of food can illustrate this for us. The act of eating is comparatively simple, yet it is but the beginning of a highly complex process of metabolism by which the food is assimilated and distributed throughout the organism. The believer's faith-reply to the word of God initiates a complex process in which the trust and love of the will are aroused, the temperament is stimulated, man is moved to fashion his whole life according to the challenging summons of God speaking through his representative—the minister of the word.[57] The analogy could also be stretched to apply to the preacher, who, as a dedicated and responsible cook, feeds the Christian family nutritious meals, milk for the young, solid food for the mature.[58] And since faith is a life process,[59] it implies growth, and this necessitates a steady feeding with the word of God.

It should not be assumed that the growth in faith which preaching aims at nourishing necessarily implies that when the preacher preaches on the Trinity, Incarnation, Transfiguration, Passion, or Resurrection, he does so with the express intention of getting the people to go home and do something about it. The preacher intends to assist the strengthening of his listeners' assent in faith, to help lead them to a more personal encounter with Him Who is Truth, to a loving submission to His will which entails a more Christlike way of life. Good works almost always accompany this progress in faith, yet the immediate concern of preaching must be the strengthening of assent, the willing acceptance of faith. To persuade people to particular actions without bothering about this indispensable foundation would be like building a house on sand.[60]

Although the instrument wielded by the preacher to accomplish his sacred goal is "keener than any two-edged sword" (Heb 4:12), nevertheless, the favorability of his listener's response will depend primarily on God's grace and his hearer's cooperation. Preaching aims at initiating the supernatural process by which the whole man is disposed to cooperate generously with the flow of God's grace. As Saint Paul said: "I have planted, Apollos watered, but God has given the growth" (I Cor 3:6). This growth is called salvation, or a greater union of the soul with God, which in turn redounds to the glory of God. It is thus that preaching is said to accomplish its purpose.

Preaching, therefore, is part of the integral mystery of Christ, an actual prolongation of the mission of the Word made flesh, with the same goal, man's salvation. Theologically, preaching is the point of contact between the objective and subjective orders of redemption, the ordinary conduit through which the saving grace of Christ is channeled to adult men. It should be noted that it is never entirely inefficacious, for it can be effective of condemnation as well as salvation. Our Lord's forceful words: "He who hears you, hears me: and he who rejects you, rejects me; and he who rejects me, rejects him who sent me" (Lk 10:16), cannot be taken lightly. Preaching, therefore, is not only salutary for those who receive it, but also condemnatory for those who refuse it. God's word forces a man to take a stand in relation to the plan of God proposed to him by this sacred ministry. This stand is inevitable since the object presented to him is God Himself, and a man cannot be indifferent towards divine values. Man, therefore, can accept Christ in faith, or reject Him. It is the function of preaching to propose this momentous choice to his freedom [61] and convey the grace that ignites man's loving response in faith.

NOTION OF "MISSION"

God who "wills that all men be saved and come to the knowledge of the truth" (I Tim 2:4), "who in many and various ways spoke in times past to the fathers by the prophets" (Heb 1:1), when the fullness of time had come sent his Son, the Word made flesh, anointed by the Holy Spirit, to preach the gospel to the poor. . . . Just as Christ was sent by the Father, so also he sent the apostles, filled with the Holy Spirit. This he did that, by preaching the gospel to every creature, they might proclaim that the Son of God, by his death and resurrection, had freed us from the power of Satan and from death, and brought us into the kingdom of his Father.[62]

Bishops, as successors of the apostles, receive from the Lord, to whom was given all power in heaven and on earth, the mission to teach all nations and to preach the gospel to every creature, so that all men may attain to salvation by faith, baptism and the fulfillment of the commandments. To fulfill this mission, Christ the Lord promised the Holy Spirit from heaven, by whose power they would be witnesses to him before the nations and peoples and kings even to the ends of the earth.[63]

Christ, whom the Father has sanctified and sent into the world, has through his apostles, made their successors, partakers of his consecration and his mission . . . Priests . . . are consecrated to preach the gospel . . . Partakers of the function of Christ, the sole Mediator, on their level of ministry, they announce the divine word to all." [64]

These Council texts accentuate the vital link between the preaching of a priest, his bishop, the apostles, the Holy Spirit, Christ and the Father. The faithful believe the revealed truth spoken by the ministers of the word because they believe the testimony of God revealing himself through them. The preacher's witness is not a self-testimony, for he traces his authority right back to God, and the fulfillment of God's mandate to preach the gospel is called his "mission." It is called "canonical" mission insofar as it is exercised according to the norm of authority instituted by Christ in his Church. This mission is rooted in the very depths of the mystery of the Trinitarian processions. It originates in the Father and is destined to return to Him. Revelation indicates a logical sequence of facts: the Father, the generation of the Word, the procession of the Spirit, the temporal mission of the Word in the Incarnation, the temporal mission of the Spirit at Pentecost, the mission of the Church in the person of the apostles and their successors, and finally the Father who is all in all. The mission therefore prolongs the process of love in the Trinity, is a product of its emergence, of its bursting forth into time. There is in reality only one missionary, Christ, and only one mission, Christ's. The mission of the Spirit is its other aspect, its complement and ful-fillment. Christ's mission takes two forms, a personal form which consisted in achieving mankind's salvation for the glory of God and in founding the Church, and a collective form which is to last until the end of time and is the gathering together of all things and of all men in the sanctifying love of the Father, the regrouping of mankind into one single divine family. Since in the last analysis there is only one mission, Christ's, the Church alone can be "sent," missioned, since she alone is the Body and Bride of Christ, Christ fulfilling him-self through the centuries. In the accomplishment of this mission, the Church is both the means and the end. She is the means by which the faith is spread and she works at the building up of her own body to her own fulfillment until she reaches the mature stature of the fullness of Christ.[65]

Our Lord was profoundly conscious of the mission given him by the Father. When the Pharisees reproached him: "Thou bearest wit-ness to thyself. Thy witness is not true," he replied: "Even if I bear witness to myself, my witness is true, because I know where I came from and where I go . . . I am not alone, but with me is he who sent me, the Father . . . It is I who bear witness to myself, and he who sent me, the Father, bears witness to me" (Jn 8:14, 16, 18). "I have not spoken on my own authority, but he who sent me, the Father, has commanded me what I should say, and what I should declare. The things, therefore, that I speak, I speak as the Father has bidden me" (Jn 12:49-50). "I preach only what the Father has taught me" (Jn 8:28). The Father had already given testimony of his Son's mandate at the Transfiguration: "And there came a voice out of the cloud, saying: This is my beloved Son; hear him" (Lk 9:35).

The Holy Spirit, proceeding from the Father and the Son, would be sent to strengthen the apostles to accomplish the mission given by Christ. "But the Advocate, the Holy Spirit whom the Father will send in my name, he will teach you all things, and bring to your mind whatever I have said to you" (Jn 14:26). "When the spirit of truth has come, he will teach you all the truth. For he will not speak on his own authority, but whatever he will hear he will speak, and the things that are to come he will declare to you. He will glorify me, because he will receive of what is mine, and will declare it to you" (Jn 16: 13-15). "When the Advocate has come, whom I will send you from the Father, the Spirit of truth who proceeds from the Father, he will bear witness concerning me. And you also bear witness, be-cause from the beginning you are with me" (Jn 15:26-27).

Therefore it is fundamentally the eternal Father who, from the pro-found depths of the Godhead, speaks his divine Word into the world through the Incarnation. The mission of his Son is prolonged in his

Church through the Holy Spirit, who speaks through the ministers of the word, making their gospel message to be, as it truly is, the word of God.[66] Thus there are three, the Father, the Son, and the Holy Spirit, who reveal themselves through the Church's preaching. As John said: "There are three that bear witness, the Father, the Word, and the Holy Spirit, and these three are one" (I Jn 5:7).[67] Where this Trinitarian testimony is absent by reason of the lack of an authentic mission to preach in the name of Christ as the commissioned organ of the Holy Spirit for the glory of the Father, that preaching is not preaching but "sounding brass and tinkling cymbal" (I Cor 13:1); human speech, but not the word of God.

Probably no theologian has been more emphatic in insisting on the essential place the canonical mission holds in the ministry of preaching than Fr. Augustine Rock. His opinion rests upon such stalwart columns as St. Thomas Aquinas and St. Albert the Great. "If preaching is to announce the word of God," says Fr. Rock, "then if one be not sent by God, how can he be said to preach? His words are his own, not the word of God." [68] As St. Thomas insisted: "No one, no matter how great his learning, or how great his sanctity, unless sent by God or by a prelate is able to preach." [69] Therefore, anyone who is called on to preach does so neither in his own name, nor by reason of his theological knowledge, but solely by reason of the mandate which he has received from the lawful teaching authority. His faculty to preach always remains subject to that authority, and it is never exercised in its own right or independently.[70] "No interior urge to preach the gospel, no sense of a divine call, no sacred order or religious profession, can make up for the lack of proper authorization." [71] The canonical mission, therefore, is by no means a mere accidental element in preaching the word of God. It is so essential that without it there can be no question of preaching in the true and proper sense of the term.

Lest anyone object that such a notion is too juridical, it is well to mention that it is founded on the traditional interpretation of Paul's rhetorical question to the Romans: "How are they to believe him whom they have not heard? And how are they to hear, if no one preaches? And how are men to preach unless they be sent?" (Rom 10:14-15). Both St. Thomas and Martin Luther were equally emphatic in declaring that whoever should pretend to preach without being sent by God, i.e., without an authorized mission, would be in a class with the false prophets. Luther, who wrote his commentary as a Catholic in 1515-16, goes so far as to declare: "This is the mighty arrow that strikes down the heretics." [72] That Luther never abandoned his doctrine regarding the necessity of a proved mission is clear from his writings against the Anabaptists, whom he accused of prophesying without being divinely sent. To distinguish himself from the "false prophets" of Zwickau,

Luther invoked his own title of "doctor", thus cloaking his preaching with a certain specious legitimacy.[73]

Since Christ bequeathed his salvific message to the Church to be proclaimed until the Parousia, the traditional teaching of the Church has been that the ministry of the word is "the principal function of bishops," [74] the successors of the apostles.

But since the bishops could never fulfill their teaching duty alone, due both to the vastness of the areas they must evangelize and to the multiple tasks of their episcopal ministry, they therefore enlist the help of priests, to whom they confide the task of preaching the divine word to the people. This episcopal delegation of the preaching ministry to priests has a long tradition behind it, as Fr. Doronzo has shown:

> Public preaching in churches, which was originally reserved to bishops as the principal duty of their pastoral care (as Chrysostom emphatically asserted), gradually was conceded on occasion also to priests, as is shown by the Council of Ancyra in the year 314, which enumerated 'giving the sermon to the people' among the priest's duties. In the West, it was not until near the end of the fourth century, mainly through the works of Augustine, that the praxis was introduced of committing to priests the ordinary function of preaching in church. In the subsequent age the custom became so widespread that Isidore of Seville did not hesitate to list the celebration of the Eucharist and preaching the divine word as the principal duties of priests.[75]

The question naturally comes to mind: can the bishop commission only those with the power of sacred Orders to preach in his stead, and if so, is there then a definite link between preaching the word of God and the sacrament of Orders? Church history attests to the fact that laymen did preach, especially in the first centuries.[76] Origen is a classic example of this,[77] yet it remained essentially a rarity and certainly never became commonplace. Santamaria attributed such isolated cases to extraordinary divine charismata rather than to an exercise of the Church's ordinary teaching office.[78] Although this not too frequent praxis gradually became almost non-existent, it was not until the year 1215, at the Fourth General Council of the Lateran, that laymen were definitely excluded from the office of preaching.[79] Our present Code of Canon Law prohibits preaching in church by laymen.[80]

Pius XII explicitly stated that a layman could receive a canonical mission to teach religion, but was quick to point out that even though his mandate from the bishop might on occasion be the same as the priest's, nevertheless, the apostolate of the one is lay and that of the other is priestly, *vi muneris sacerdotalis*.[81] If this difference exists in the performance of the same canonical mission, v.g., to teach catechism, it follows that there is a vast difference between the layman's mission to teach religion and the priest's mission to preach the word of God.

This difference would not seem to consist merely in the Code's prohibition of preaching in church on the part of laymen,[82] nor on the Council of Trent's decree: "If anyone says that all Christians have the power to administer the word and all the sacraments, let him be anathema." [83] Indeed, it is significant that the fathers of the council united the ministry of preaching with that of the sacraments, and this could be a clue to uncovering the theological answer to the problem of an essential link between preaching and sacred Orders. The mission to preach is given to priests and not to laymen precisely because the former possess something which the latter do not have. The most logical "something" would seem to be the sacrament of Orders, whereby the subject is stamped with a sacred fitness that enables him to receive a mandate to preach. The sacrament of Orders would thus be conceived as a *conditio sine qua non* for the exercise of the preaching ministry.

The conferral of a special power in conjunction with the mission of preaching is not without a Biblical basis. This is perfectly clear in I Tim 1:12: "I give thanks to him who infused power (*endunamosanti*) into me, Christ Jesus our Lord. I thank him for judging me worthy of this trust and appointing me to his service." The aorist *endunamosanti* refers to a definite moment of past time: Paul's vocation on the Damascus Road. There he received not only a mission but also the power which made its fulfillment possible. The new English Bible's paraphrase renders the sense well: "I thank him who has made me equal to the task." This power is without doubt that which Jesus promised to his apostles when he sent them to preach (Mt 28:28-30; Acts 1:7-8). Because the apostles as founders of the Church enjoyed special graces, one cannot infer that what was given them is necessarily the property of every preacher. Paul, however, by his use of the plural in I Thess 2:4 and II Cor 4:7, indicates that graces analogous to his own have been conferred on his assistants. It is an awareness of this power within him that he tries to arouse in Timothy when the difficulties of the latter's task seem almost to overwhelm him: "I remind you to rekindle the gift of God which is within you through the laying on of my hands" (II Tim 1:6).[84] It is not improbable that Paul is here referring to the sacraments of Orders, as he had previously admonished Timothy: "Do not neglect the grace that is in thee, granted to thee by reason of prophecy with the laying on of hands of the presbyterate" (I Tim 4:14).

Although it has not yet been ascertained as to just what might be the precise nature of any existing relationship between the sacerdotal character and the preaching of the word, nevertheless, the traditional testimony, admitting but a few exceptions, that only those possessing the sacrament of Orders are actually commissioned to preach God's word is a strong argument in favor of an existing relationship, *ab esse ad posse valet illatio.*

Theologians are not in accord in distinguishing the powers conferred on the Church by Christ. Some favor a two-fold division: Orders and jurisdiction; others prefer a three-fold division: Orders, jurisdiction and teaching.[85] Pius XII explicitly spoke of the bipartite distinction, but in such a way as to include the functions of teaching and governing within the structure of the power of jurisdiction:

> Christ granted His apostles a two-fold power: first, the priestly power to consecrate, which was given in its fullness to all the apostles: second, the power to teach and govern, that is, to communicate to men in God's name the infallible truth which binds them, and to establish the rules which regulate Christian life. These powers of the apostles they passed on to the pope and bishops. The bishops, through the ordination of priests, transmit to others to a determined extent the power to consecrate; the power to teach and govern belongs to the pope and bishops.[86]

The power of Orders, therefore, enables the recipient to participate directly in God's sanctification of the faithful, while the power of jurisdiction gives the right to rule, guide and teach the faithful.

Although this distinction of powers is useful in theology, we should never lose sight of the basic unity of all of them in the Church's single power to continue the mission of Christ in the world. Fr. Charles Davis insists on this point, and while maintaining that the canonical mission is the necessary condition for the exercise of preaching, he holds that preaching is an exercise of the power of Orders. Fr. Paul Boyle also sees in the sacrament of Orders "the radical power to preach authoritatively." [88] Fr. Davis cites Scheeben as a possible original source in the formulation of his own opinion.[89] Scheeben held that bishops have the plenitude of teaching authority *vi ordinis,* and the sacred Orders conferred on priests and deacons equip them with the connatural power required to preach as fit cooperators of the bishop. He conceived the canonical mission in the traditional sense, i.e., as the episcopal mandate to announce in an official· capacity the salvific message entrusted to the bishops' care by Jesus Christ.[90]

In this connection, one can readily see the value of not stressing the traditional division of powers in the Church but rather of accentuating their unified interaction. Preaching serves as a universal organ of the ecclesiastical magisterium in propagating and strengthening the faith, and thus it coincides with the purpose of the power of Orders, namely, the sanctification of the faithful. Therefore, although preaching is commonly situated under the magisterium in the classic division of powers in the Church, and the magisterium in turn under the power of jurisdiction, nevertheless, preaching is also linked to the power of Orders by reason of their common purpose—the sanctification of souls. Apparently this was clear to St. Thomas: "Preaching and hearing confessions are dependent upon both jurisdiction and Orders." [91] The Angelic Doctor based the relationship of preaching to sacred Orders on his conception of preaching as a sacred ministry: "Ministers, however, impart grace in various ways, through the administration of the sacraments of grace . . . and also through the exortation of sermons." [92] Fr. Rock is very emphatic in his interpretation of St. Thomas' thought on this matter: "Without sacred Orders, preaching cannot exist, for the character of Orders empowers a man to preach just as much as it enables him to consecrate." [93]

A word of caution however is due here against any opinion that might over-emphasize or insist solely on the conferring of the episcopal or priestly character as constituting the recipient as an authentic teacher. A formidable canonical objection, already voiced by Lorenz Schnell [94] and reiterated by Wilhelm Bartz,[95] thwarts any facile solution of the problem. The difficulty is this: if the power of Orders, either in its plenitude, the episcopacy, or in the priesthood, constituted the subject as an authentic teacher, be it actually or radically, then how can the fact be explained that Canon Law grants the power to teach authentically even to those who have not received episcopal ordination: an elected pope,[96] even if he has not yet been ordained a bishop; cardinals who are not bishops;[97] a nominated residential bishop even before his consecration; [98] and prelates nullius? [99] Even if the foregoing be considered as "privileges," the problem of an absent episcopal character remains. If one were to reply that all of the aforementioned are usually priests, and therefore have at least the radical power to teach, nevertheless, the core of the problem remains and was envisaged by Pius XII when he said:

> Even if a layman were elected pope, he could accept the election only if he were fit for ordination and willing to be ordained. But the power to teach and govern, as well as the charism of infallibility, would be granted to him from the very moment of his acceptance, even before his ordination.[100]

By way of conclusion, therefore, there seems to be present a theological as well as historical basis for radicating the preaching act in the power of Orders. Once it is admitted that preaching is a divinely chosen instrument of faith, the very frequency of its use in the Church would link it quite normally to the Mystical Body's ordinary divinely established agency of grace, namely, the priesthood. The power of Orders could then be conceived as fitting the priest to be a connatural instrument in the hands of Christ for the ministry of the word, similiarly as it does for the ministry of the sacraments. The weight of theological tradition tends to favor such an interpretation; at the same time, it must be admitted that the nature of any existing bond between preaching and sacred Orders is in too embryonic a stage of theological development to allow for a definite satisfactory solution at the moment.

PREACHING AND THE SACRAMENTS

Pius XI called preaching: "the sacrament of sacraments, a kind of transcendental sacrament." [101] He certainly did not intend by this to make preaching some sort of eighth sacrament, but rather that the ministry of the word is very much like the sacraments in nature and operation, remaining however *sui generis,* similar, e.g., to our saying that the seven sacraments are similar to the Sacrament par excellence, the Incarnate Word.[102] Preaching and the sacraments, both distinct species, convene in genus by being the points of contact between the objective redemption and the salvation of the individual believer.

Striking similarities do exist between the two. Most of the sacraments have the same ordinary minister as preaching, namely, a bishop or priest; both are channels of grace to the recipient who places no obstacle in their way; both work through the casuality of a conscious minister's spoken words; both were instituted by Christ; both are special organs of faith.[103]

However the dissimilarities are just as numerous. The sacraments cause sanctifying grace, while preaching is a divine appeal to men after the manner of an actual grace, with special reference to the virtue of faith;[104] the sacraments, except infant baptism, suppose faith in the recipient, while preaching is directed to the living and dead faith of believers as well as to those without any faith at all; the sacraments have an *ex opere operato* efficacy in themselves, while preaching makes no such claim, and in fact is more dependent on the activity of the minister. As Cardinal Suhard said: "The efficacy of the sacramental rites does not depend on the minister. He may be a sinner or an ignoramus; the effect is nevertheless completely produced." [105]

> All that is necessary for a valid sacrament is exactly determined. No matter how careless and unworthy the priest, if he administers the sacrament correctly, it comes into existence with all its power of causing grace. With preaching, it is left to the preacher to form the word of God. It depends on him how far a sermon is the genuine word of God. His activity determines whether the word of God is presented in its full richness or in an impoverished form.[106]

Although they differ essentially, nevertheless, preaching and the sacraments are intimately related to each other. The sacraments are truly "mysteries—mysteries which can be penetrated only by faith. And faith needs to be clarified and formed by preaching the word." [107] Preaching, therefore, functions as a *mystagogy,* disposing the faithful to celebrate the sacraments more fruitfully and to participate more fully in the encounter with God in the holy sacrifice.[108]

RELEVANCE OF "MISSION" TO SUNDAY SERMON

This last consideration leads us to the final section of this paper—
the relevance of "mission" to the Sunday sermon as it is part of the
liturgical celebration of the Mass. Our starting point is the *Constitution on the Liturgy:*

> Before men can came to the liturgy, they must be called to
> faith and to conversion: "How then are they to call upon him in
> whom they have not yet believed? But how are they to believe
> him whom they have not heard? And how are they to hear if no
> one preaches? And how are men to preach unless they be sent?"
> (Rom 10:14-15). Therefore the Church announces the good
> tidings of salvation to those who do not believe, so that all men
> may know the true God and Jesus Christ whom He has sent, and
> may be converted from their ways, doing penance. To believers
> also, the church must ever preach faith and penance; she must
> prepare them for the sacraments, teach them to observe all that
> Christ has commanded.[109]

> In the liturgy, God speaks to his people and Christ is still
> proclaiming his gospel.[110]

> The sermon is part of the liturgical service . . . its character
> should be that of a proclamation of God's wonderful works in the
> history of salvation, the mystery of Christ, ever made present and
> active within us, especially in the celebration of the liturgy.[111]

> By means of the homily, the mysteries of the faith and the
> guiding principles of the Christian life are expanded from the
> sacred text . . . the homily, therefore, is to be highly esteemed as
> part of the liturgy itself.[112]

> The liturgy of the word and the Eucharistic liturgy are so
> closely connected with each other that they form but one single
> act of worship. Accordingly this sacred Synod strongly urges
> pastors of souls that when instructing the faithful, they insistently
> teach them to take their part in the entire Mass.

The Mass plants the divine plan of salvation, "the good tidings of
the unfathomable riches of Christ" (Ephes 3:8), in our very midst; it
links past salvation history with the present and even projects the
believer into the future realization of the whole mystery of Christ:
"For as often as you shall eat of this bread and drink this cup, you
proclaim the death of the Lord, until he comes" (I Cor 11:26). The
Mass is the sacred time and place, par excellence, the divine milieu
for the proclamation of the word of God. Although the Mass makes
present here and now the whole redeeming mystery of Christ, its effect
upon those present is not automatic.

> Our minds and hearts need to be opened to it so that we may
> lay hold of its saving effect. To profit from the Mass, we need to
> have, in the traditional phrase, the right dispositions, and while
> no doubt there is more than one way open to people to acquire
> them, yet it is one of the principal functions of the ministry
> of the word to do so. We may not rush into the presence of
> the Lord. It is not only irreverent but unprofitable. The Great
> Action is so rich, so many-sided, that we need to be helped to
> grasp its significance not once but again and again. The liturgical

sermon is thus the bridge between the mystery of Christ proclaimed by God's word in the first part of the Mass and the
making present of that mystery in deed and in truth in the second.
The Word who speaks in the first is as it were incarnated again
for us in the second.[114] Faith, awakened and made meaningful
by the service of the word, is the vital environment of the Mass
and sacraments—another reason why Christ has entrusted the
ministry of both word and sacrament to the same office.[115]

Just as Christ inflamed the hearts of the disciples on the road to
Emmaus as he spoke and explained the Scriptures to them, enlighten-
ing their faith so that "they recognized him in the breaking of the
bread" (Lk 24:35), so too, the word of God proclaimed at Mass
stimulates the dialogue between the believer and his God and thus
readies the heart for the holy communion of love in the sacrament of
the Eucharist. The two disciples were discouraged. Our Lord did not
rebuke them, he did not directly encourage them, he *enlightened* them,
i.e., he put the events of those apparently tragic days into a *faith
perspective*. So, too, the minister of the word strives to relate the
events, the problems and trials of the people of God into the perspective of the redeeming cross and resurrection.[116] His preaching fans
the believer's embers of faith, hope and love, and thus readies him for
the heart to heart encounter with the Lord of *history* who comes now
in the Mass in *mystery,* a pledge of his coming again in *majesty.*

This means putting the life situation of people into a faith-perspective, i.e., their problems, trials, worries, sufferings, joys, routine, etc.,
should be related to their "growing up in Christ." They must pass
through the Paschal mystery of living, suffering, dying, rising. This in
no way means that we "explain away" the trials of life, but rather
try to see them in relationship to Christ. Thus, my strengthening of
faith's assent will not cause my amputated leg to return, her cancer to
disappear, his homosexual tendency to vanish, their "booby-prize"
son to hit the honor role, etc., but it should give me the supernatural
internal frame of reference necessary to carry this cross. It will not
remove the cross or perhaps even the shadow of the cross, but it
should give me the faith-muscled shoulders to bear up under that
cross and even transform it into redemptive currency, for my faith
assures me that Calvary is a necessary prelude to the empty tomb,
the darkness of Good Friday must precede the bright light of Easter
morn—in my life, "Christian", just as in Christ's life, otherwise I am
like him in name only but not in reality.

I believe we have a good analogy to preaching's deepening of faith-
assent in what transpires at Lourdes during the blessing of the sick.

Thousands make a faith-filled, hope-full petition to be cured, but
it is seldom that anyone is actually cured. Yet it is evident to anyone
with eyes to see that no one leaves that faith-hope-setting the same.
The sickness remains, but God has spoken. He said, "No!" He wants

to prolong His suffering in them, "to fill up those things still wanting in the sufferings of Christ." The faith-assent is seen on the faces of the sick, faces that seem to say "resignation, peace, God wills it," and they mean it, because it means something to them now, or it has more meaning to them now.

It is thus that a strengthened faith-perspective enables the believer to change the "*d*" of every "*d*isappointment" into a capital "*H*"; now read it: "*H*is-appointment." This does not solve problems, but it does make them bearable, livable, even sanctifying, because they are now meaningful, made so by a more penetrating faith-vision.

It seems to me to be an inside-to-the-out (immanent) transformation that takes place when our faith is strengthened. Perhaps the life-situation remains the same *materialiter,* but *formaliter* it is completely changed; it is "trans-substantiated."

The question was once asked Fr. N. Mailloux, O.P.: "Does *understanding* a bad habit or conflict help one to solve it?" The noteworthy psychologist replied: "One does not change *because* he understands, but one understands mostly *because* he has *already* undergone a deep transformation in his personal attitudes, i.e., the final emergence of a solution into consciousness after a long struggle presupposes the surmounting of persistant resistances and the developing of more mature emotional attitudes." Analogically speaking, I think that a regular diet of solid preaching does the same thing in the believer's personality.[117]

The preacher of the cultic word should never forget that he speaks not in his own name, for he proclaims God's word as a messenger from God. He is not primarily a personal witness to the deeds he announces, as were the prophets and apostles. His message comes from within the Church, and he is sent by the Church to accomplish this sacred mission. Just as a priest is empowered to pronounce the words of consecration, so he is commissioned to announce the word of God. As an "other Christ," he brings Christ's authentic *word,* just as he brings Christ's authentic *food.* It is not out of mere courtesy that at pontifical Masses the preacher asks the blessing of the bishop. He seeks the bishop's approval to speak in his name, and his commission to do so links him with the apostles, the Holy Spirit, Christ, and the Father. It is thus that the homily is an *ecclesial* act, expressing the *hierarchial structure* of the Church, a *sign* of the *mission* Christ commanded his Church to fulfill "even unto the consummation of the world" (Mt 28:20).

By baptism, every believer is a temple, God's dwelling place, and the *activity* of the believer participates in this *liturgical* character of his being. He worships God in himself; he is a priest officiating in the temple of his own body; his life becomes a living sacrifice of worshipful love of God. Just as the believer offers worship to God by his faithful response to his responsibilities, so the priest-believer offers worship to God by responding faithfully to his primary responsibility —to preach the gospel. The minister of the word is never an absolute, never autonomous—always the voice of God. His message is "personalized" in delivery, but the force which makes it *the power of God for salvation"* (Rom 1:16) stems from the divine efficacy, and his mission is like the temporal missions of the Son and the Holy Spirit.[118]

FOOTNOTES

[1] Z. Alszeghy and M. Flick, "Il problema teologico della predicazione," *Gregorianum* 40 (1959), 671-744.

[2] J. A. Jungmann, *Die Frohbotschaft und unsere Glaubensverkundigung* (Regensburg, 1936) Introduction.

[3] Pius XII, *Mediator Dei*, AAS 39 (1947) 529.

[4] *Constitution on the Liturgy*, n. 35.

[5] *Ibid.*, n. 52.

[6] J. J. von Allmen, "Semaine romande de theologie pastorale," *Verbum Caro* (1955) 137.

K. Barth, *La proclamation de l'Evangile* (Delachaux et Niestle) 25-26.

E. Schillebeeckx, *Christ the Sacrament of the Encounter with God* (Sheed and Ward, N.Y., 1963) 185.

[7] J. L. Allgeier, *The Canonical Obligation of Preaching in Parish Churches* (Washington, D. C., 1949) 1.

[8] A. Dulles, "Protestant Preacher and Prophetic Mission," *Theological Studies* 21 (1960) 545.

[9] Benedict XV, *Humani generis Redemptionem*, AAS 9 (1917) 305-06.

[10] *Extractum e Pontificali Romano* (Malines, 1933) 35.

[11] P. Charles, "Reflexions sur la theologie du sermon," *N R T* 69 (1947) 581-82.

[12] *Constitution on the Church*, n. 5.

[13] *Acts* 2:14-40.

[14] *Acts* 4:12.

[15] *Acts* 2:9-10.

[16] *John* 4:2.

[17] *II Tim.* 4:17.

[18] C. Spicq, *The Mystery of Godliness* (Chicago, 1954) 94.

[19] *Concilium Tridentinum*, Sess. 5, de lectione et praedicatione (CT 5. 242).

[20] *Constitution on the Church*, n. 17.

[21] John XXIII, *Al saluto scambiato*, AAS 50 (1958) 916.

[22] John XXIII, *Catholicus sacerdos*, AAS 52 (1960) 240.

[23] J. L. Allgeier, *Op. cit.*, 51-54.

[24] A. Bea, "The Pastoral Value of the Word of God in the Sacred Liturgy," *The Assisi Papers*, 87.

[25] John XXIII, *Al saluto scambiato*, AAS 50 (1958) 918.

[26] *Constitution on the Church*, n. 28.

[27] Paul VI, *Ecclesiam suam*, AAS (1964).

[28] J. B. Montini, Letter to the Nat'l Congress of Montpellier 1954, *Le Pretre Ministre de la Parole* (Paris, 1954) 6.

[29] F. X. Legrand, "The Constitution 'De Ecclesia' and the Evangelization of the World," *Christ to the World*, 10 (1965) 119.

[30] J. Danielou, "Parole de Dieu et mission de L'Eglise," *Le Pretre Ministre de la Parole*, 42.

[31] *Constitution on the Liturgy*, n. 5.

[32] Y. B. Tremel, "Serviteurs de la Parole," *Lumiere et vie* 9 (1960) 9.

[33] *Mark* 16:15-16.

[34] *Rom.* 10:18.

[35] C. Spicq, *Op. cit.*, 75.

[36] *La Sainte Bible* (Paris, 1956) 1609, b.

[37] Benedict XV, *Negli anni scorsi*, AAS 10 (1918) 93.

[38] *Constitution on the Church*, n. 1.

[39] Benedict XV, *E bello il nome*, AAS 13 (1921) 96.

[40] P. Hitz, *L'Annonce Missionaire de l'Evangile* (Paris, 1954) 82.

[41] J. Murphy-O'Connor, *Paul on Preaching* (Sheed and Ward, N.Y., 1964) 137-38.

[42] Alszegy-Flick, *Art. cit.*, 742.

[43] L. J. Suenens, *The Gospel to Every Creature* (Newman, 1957) 43.

[44] Benedict XV, *E bello il nome*, AAS 13 (1921) 94-95.

[45] F. X. Arnold, *Serviteurs de la Foi* (Tournai, 1957) 2.

[46] *Ibid.*, 3.

[47] St. Ambrose, *De Spiritu Sancto* 1.3.42 (Ml 16.714).
St. Augustine, *Epistola 98, Ad Bonifacium*, CSEL 34. 531.

[48] *Rituale Romanum*, tit. 2, cap. 2 (Rome, 1952) 17.

[49] *Summa Theologica* 3, q. 61, art. 4 (PT 4. 268).

[50] *Constitution on the Liturgy*, n. 59.

[51] *Concilium Tridentinum*, Sess. 6, de justificatione (CT 5. 794); (Mansi 33.8 35).

[52] Murphy-O'Connor, *Op. cit.*, 126.

[53] *Rom.* 10:17.

[54] C. Davis, "The Theology of Preaching," *Clergy Review* 45 (1960) 535.

[55] M. Cordovani, "Il Sacerdote Predicatore," *Enciclopedia del Sacerdozio* (Florence, 1953) 1067.

[56] *La Sainte Bible*, 1492, a.

[57] O. Semmelroth, *The Preaching Word* (Herder and Herder, 1965) 195-97.

[58] *I Cor.* 3:1-2; *Heb.* 5:12-13.

[59] *Rom.* 1:17.

[60] W. Toohey, "Is Preaching Merely Sacred Rhetoric," *A E R* 145 (1961) 159.

[61] D. Grasso, Nuovi apporti alla teolgia della predicazione," *Gregorianum* 44 (1963) 102.

[62] *Constitution on the Liturgy*, nn. 5,6.

[63] *Constitution on the Church*, n. 24.

[64] *Ibid.*, n. 28.

[65] L. and A. Retif, *The Church's Mission in the World* (Hawthorn, N.Y., 1962) 90-91.

[66] *II Cor.* 5:20; *I Thess.* 2:13.

[67] L. Claussen, "The Mystery of Preaching," *The Word* (Kenedy, N.Y., 1964) 188-89.

[68] A. Rock, *Unless They Be Sent* (Dubuque, 1953) III.

[69] *Quaestiones Quodlibetales*, Quodlibetum 12, q. 18, art. 27, (PT 9. 628).

[70] Pius XII, *Si diligis*, AAS 46 (1954) 314-15.

[71] J. McVann, *The Canon Law of Sermon Preaching* (New York, 1940) 60.

[72] *Scholia* on Rom. 1:17 (WA 56, 422-23).

[73] Dulles, *Art. cit.*, 547.
Y. Congar, *Vrai et fausse reforme* (Paris, 1950) 509-20.

[74] *Concilium Tridentinum*, Sess. 5, de lectione et praedicatione (CT 5. 242).
J. D. Mansi, *Sacrorum conciliorum nova et amplissima collectio*, 33. Sess. 5, De reformatione, c. 2 (Paris, 1902).

[75] E. Doronzo, *De Ordine* 1 (Milwaukee, 1957) 960.

[76] Y. Congar, *Lay People in the Church* (Westminster, Md., 1957) 291-98.

[77] J. Quasten, *Patrology*, 2 (Westminster, Md., 1953) 39.

[78] F. Santamaria, *Comentarios al Codigo Canonico*, 4 (Madrid, 1920-22) 195.

[79] *Con. Lat. IV*, De haeret. 3 (Mansi 22. 990).

[80] *Codex Iuris Canonici*, can. 1342, parag. 2.

[81] Pius XII, *Six ans se sont*, AAS 49 (1957) 924-25.

[82] *Codex Iuris Canonici*, can. 1342, parag. 2.

83 *Con. Trid.,* Sess. 7, De Sacramentis in genera (CT 5. 995); (Mansi 33. 53).

84 Murphy-O'Connor, *Op. cit.,* 81-82.

85 T. Zapelena, *De Ecclesia Christi,* 2 (Rome, 1954) 151-71.

86 Pius XII, *Six ans se sont,* AAS 49 (1957) 924.

87 Davis, *Art. cit.,* 530.

88 P. Boyle, "The Moral Obligation of Preaching," *Proceedings of the Catholic Homiletic Society,* Chicago (1960) 23-32:

89 Davis, *Art. cit.,* 546.

90 W. Bartz, "Le Magistere de l'Eglise d'apres Scheeben," *L'Ecclesiologie au XIXe Siecle* (Paris, 1960) 313-19.

91 St. Thomas, *Contra Impugnantes Dei Cultum et Religionem,* cap. 4 (PT 15. 17).

92 St. Thomas, *In Epistolam ad Romanos,* cap. 1, lect. 5 (PT 13. 12-13).

93 Rock, *Op. cit.,* 133.

94 L. Schnell, "Die Gliederung der Kirchengewalten," *Theol. Quartalschrift,* 71 (1889) 387-440.

95 Bartz, *Art. cit.,* 316.

96 *Codex Iuris Canonici,* can. 219.

97 *Ibid.,* can. 239, parag. 1, n. 3.

98 *Ibid.,* can. 349, parag. 1, n. 1.

99 *Ibid.,* can. 323, parag. 1.

100 Pius XII, *Six ans se sont,* AAS 49 (1957) 924.

101 Pius XI, *Il Santo Padre affermava, Discorsi* 1 (1922-28) 352.

102 *Summa Theologica,* 3, q. 60, art. 6 (PT 4. 263.64).

103 *Constitution on the Liturgy,* nn. 9, 59.

104 Davis, *Art. cit.,* 535-36.

105 *The Church Today,* The Collected Writings of Emmanuel Cardinal Suhard (Chicago, 1953) 245.

106 Davis, *Art. cit.,* 537.

107 A. M. Roguet, "Liturgical Renewal and the Renewal of Preaching," *The Assisi Papers* (Collegeville, 1957) 92.

108 C. Vagaggini, *Il senso teologico della liturgia* (Rome, 1958) 683-85.

109 *Constitution on the Liturgy,* n. 9.

110 *Ibid.,* n. 33.

111 *Ibid.,* n. 35.

112 *Ibid.,* n. 52.

113 *Ibid.,* n. 56.

114 J. D. Crichton, "Liturgical Preaching," *Clergy Review* 45 (1960) 730.

115 R. Lechner, "Liturgical Preaching," *Worship* 37 (1963) 650.

116 E. Schillebeeckx, "Revelation in Word and Deed," *The Word* (Kenedy, N.Y., 1964) 264.

117 N. Mailloux, O.P., "Morality and Contemporary Psychology," *Proceedings of the Catholic Theological Society of America, 1954,* 47-66.

118 Murphy-O'Connor, *Op. cit.,* 278-79; 298-99.

BIBLIOGRAPHY

Alszeghy, Z., S.J.-Flick, M., S.J. "Il problema teologico della predicazione," *Gregorianum,* 40 (1959), 671-744.

Benedict XV, *Humani generis Redemptionem,* AAS 9 (1917) 305-17, encyclical on preaching.

Cahouet, E., O.P. "Preaching—Its Hidden Nature," *Dominicana,* 46 (1961), 104-10.

Charles, P., S.J. "Reflexions sur la theologie du sermon," *N R T,* 69 (1947), 581-604.

Crichton, J. D. "Liturgical Preaching," *The Clergy Review,* 45 (1960), 725-33.

Davis, C. "The Theology of Preaching," *The Clergy Review,* 45 (1960), 525-47.

Dulles, A., S.J. "The Protestant Preacher and the Prophetic Mission," *Theological Studies,* 21 (1960), 544-80.

Grasso, D., S.J. "Il Kerigma e la Predicazione," *Gregorianum,* 41 (1960), 424-50.

————. "Nuovi apporti alla teologia della predicazione," Gregorianum, 44 (1963), 88-118.

Hanley, R., O.M.I. *The Theology of Preaching in Modern Papal Teaching* (Catholic U. dissertation, 1964).

Hill, E., O.P. "St. Augustine's Theory and Practice of Preaching," *The Clergy Review,* 45 (1960), 589-97.

Hitz, P., C.SS.R. *To Preach the Gospel* (Sheed and Ward, N.Y., 1963).

Jungmann, J. A., S.J. *The Good News—Yesterday and Today* (W. H. Sadlier, N.Y., 1962).

The Liturgy of the Word of God—The Liturgical Press (Collegeville, 1959).

Lumiere et Vie 9 (1960), the entire no. *64*: "La Predication."

McVann, J., C.S.P. *The Canon Law of Sermon Preaching* (Paulist Press, N.Y., 1940).

Motte, J. F., O.F.M.-Dourmap, M., O.F.M.Cap. *Mission Generale, Ouevre d'Eglise* (Paris, 1957).

Murphy-O'Connor, J., O.P. *Paul on Preaching* (Sheed and Ward, N.Y., 1964).

O'Brien, I., O.P. "Preaching—a Function of Theology," *Irish Ecclesiastical Record,* 100 (1963), 80-90.

O'Shea, W., S.S. "The Sermon is Part of the Mass," *The Homiletic and Pastoral Review,* 60 (1960), 517-26.

Preaching the Liturgical Renewal—The Liturgical Conference (Washington, D.C., 1964).

Le Pretre, ministre de la Parole—Papers of the Nat'l Congress of Montpellier, France, 1954 (Paris, 1954).

The Proceedings of the Catholic Homiletic Society of America.

Retif, L. and A., *The Church's Mission in the World* (Hawthorn, N.Y., 1962)—vol. 102 of *The 20th Century Encyclopedia of Catholicism.*

Rock, A., O.P. *Unless They be Sent* (W. C. Brown, Dubuque, Iowa, 1953).

The Sacrament of Orders—The Liturgical Press (Collegeville, 1962).

Semmelroth, O., S.J. *The Preaching Word* (Herder and Herder, N.Y., 1965).

Toohey, W., C.S.C. "Is Preaching Merely Sacred Rhetoric," *American Ecclesiastical Review,* 145 (1961), 152-59.

Vatican Council II. Constitutions on *The Church* and *The Sacred Liturgy.*

The Word—Readings in Theology Series, The Canisianum, Innsbruck (P. J. Kenedy, N.Y., 1964).

THE LITURGICAL RELATIONS OF THE HOMILY

by

The Very Reverend Monsignor John J. Cassels

INTRODUCTION

To begin and carry out any discussion on the liturgical relations of the homily one should have before him, or at least keep in mind, a number of basic documents. The first of these would be the *Constitution on the Liturgy* of the Second Vatican Council. Special note must be taken of the following numbers:

No. 51. The treasures of the Bible are to be opened up more lavishly, so that richer fare may be provided for the faithful at the table of God's word. In this way a more representative portion of the Holy Scriptures will be read to the people in the course of a prescribed number of years.

No. 52. By means of the homily the mysteries of the faith and the guiding principles of the Christian life are expounded from the sacred text, during the course of the liturgical year; the homily, therefore, is to be highly esteemed as part of the liturgy itself; in fact, at those Masses which are celebrated with the assistance of the people on Sundays and feasts of obligation, it should not be omitted except for a serious reason.

No. 35. That the intimate connection between words and rites may be apparent in the liturgy:

(1) In sacred celebrations there is to be more reading from Holy Scripture, and it is to be more varied and suitable.

(2) Because the sermon is part of the liturgical service, the best place for it is to be indicated even in the rubrics, as far as the nature of the rite will allow; the ministry of preaching is to be fulfilled with exactitude and fidelity. The sermon, moreover, should draw its contents mainly from Scriptural and liturgical

sources, and its character should be that of a proclamation of God's wonderful works in the history of salvation, the mystery of Christ, ever made present and active within us, especially in the celebration of the liturgy.

(3) Instruction which is more explicitly liturgical should also be given in a variety of ways; if necessary, short directives to be spoken by the priest or proper minister should be provided within the rites themselves. But they should occur only at the more suitable moments, and be in prescribed or similar words.

(4) Bible services should be encouraged, especially on the vigils of the more solemn feasts, on some weekdays in Advent and Lent, and on Sundays and feast days. They are to be particularly commended in places where no priest is available; when this is so, a deacon or some other person authorized by the bishop should preside over the celebration.

The *second* document to keep in mind is the *Instruction on the Liturgy* of the Post-Conciliar Commission and the Sacred Congregation of Rites, promulgated on September 26, 1964. Portions of this will be considered later. The *third* document is the *American Bishops Instruction* of the same year, special attention being given to the section on Oral Interpretation.

THE HOMILY

It is impossible to give a philosophical definition of the homily. This may be very disturbing to priests and seminarians, whose principal background of thought has been of a philosophical nature. To attempt a philosophical definition of the homily would be like trying to define a *novel* or a *drama.* The best that you should expect would be a descriptive definition, which we shall attempt to give.

What is a homily? First of all it is not a catechetical instruction, although it may and should be instructive. It is not a *fervorino* or a general commentary on the Christian life or its activities. It is not an *interruption* in the Mass, which moralists, canonists and liturgists have been arguing about for centuries. In the past it has been the custom to decide what would be valid reasons to interrupt the Mass for the sermon. The Council has settled the problem by calling the sermon "part of the liturgical service." The Council also tells us that the contents of the homily should be drawn principally from Scriptural and liturgical sources and be a "proclamation of God's wonderful works in the history of salvation."

There is no one determined way in which the homily should be structured. The effectiveness of the homily might be tested by whether or not, after its delivery, it has clarified the message contained in the Scripture and liturgy of the day and the season. After the homily the Scriptures just read and their liturgical orientation should have greater meaning. The homily should be Scriptural in its language and with the language, examples and imagery of the day's selection might well be found in the homily.

The homily should include the following:

(1) A proclamation of one or another of the great redemptive themes, as contained in the Mass formulary of the day or feast. The congregation should be confronted with the great redemptive love of God in Christ, as found in the Scripture readings of the day. Other Scriptural and liturgical sources may be used to bring forth the message with every clarity.

(2) The homilist will try to show how this assembly of people, as a group and as individuals, must respond to the word of God with faith. Practical considerations taken from their lives, from the needs of the family, the community, the Church, the nation or the world should be high-lighted for them. It is here that we see the importance of knowing and understanding people and the world in which we live.

(3) A good homily has a relation or connection with the liturgical Eucharistic action to follow. Word and sacrament are intrinsically linked and this unity should be indicated in some way, explicitly or implicitly. Naturally we are anxious to avoid the dull repetition of a set form or theme. A greater knowledge of the inexhaustible riches of the Scriptures and a promise by °the Council of a cycle of Mass formularies, covering a number of years, will assist the preacher in avoiding repetition. Even with the present set of formularies and pericopes, despite their limitations, there is opportunity for great variety of theme and presentation.

KINDS OF HOMILIES

Homilies are traditionally divided into four types:

(1) *exegetical*—this is the type dear to the heart of the Fathers of the Church. It consists in explaining verse by verse the meaning of the Scriptural selection and making the application and liturgical relation;

(2) *thematic* (topical)—a theme or topic is taken out of the Scriptures of the day, the Scriptures in general or the liturgy of the day or season, illustrated through the same sources and related to the theme;

(3) *exegetical-thematic*—a greater portion of the homily explains the Scriptures and a good portion develops a theme;

(4) *thematic-exegetical*—a theme is developed and the Scriptures are explained where needed and helpful.

CURRENT PROBLEMS

Every bishop, pastor and priest, together with the whole Church, is confronted with the problem of a complete, adequate instruction of the people. With the present requirements of the homily, how does the preacher carry out the binding legislation of the Church to make certain that the people have a complete knowledge and understanding of the "things necessary for salvation"? Just as it is to be expected that future generations will follow and obey the decrees of the Second Vatican Council, so we are expected to give heed to the councils of the past.

We recall especially the decrees of the Council of Trent relative to preaching. Trent devoted chapters of the fifth and twenty-second sessions to the Word of God. The fifth session, June 17, 1546, covered the general field of pastoral obligation and canonical mission. "Preaching," said the Council, "is the chief duty of bishops." Parish priests were enjoined to teach their people either by themselves or through others. Sundays and solemn feasts were singled out as proper times to instruct their people in the things necessary for salvation. Punishments were meted out to those who neglected the ministry of the word and canonists down through the centuries have voiced opinions as to what would constitute serious matter. Most opinions centered around the idea of a pastor failing to preach for three months.

In the twenty-fourth session of Trent the bishop was instructed as to his obligation to preach in his own church and in other churches through the parish priests. Once again Sundays and feast days are mentioned as the proper times and, in addition, the priest should preach daily or thrice a week in Advent and Lent and at other times, as the bishop judged expedient. The Council declared anathema anyone who said that bishops were not superiors over the priesthood or that canonical mission was not necessary in order to be rightful ministers of the word or the sacraments. It further declared that only those candidates were to be raised to the priesthood who after careful examinations were found suitable for preaching to the people the things all should know to be saved.

The twenty-fourth session of Trent gave approval to a work that was to affect the history of the Catholic pulpit, the *Catechism of the Council of Trent,* otherwise known as the *Roman Catechism.* Older priests, especially, are well acquainted with the five great divisions of the *Roman Catechism* that became the basis for five year cycles of sermon outlines in many dioceses. The Third Council of Baltimore, ratifying the prescriptions of the Second, prescribed that the chief headings of faith and morals be explained entirely and in good order over a period of a year or two and that the *Roman Catechism* should serve as a guide. The Baltimore Council also passed strong legislation in favor of five minute sermons in addition to the reading of the gospel in the vernacular at all Masses on Sundays and feast days. Priests failing to fulfill this obligation were to be punished by the Ordinary. Baltimore also endorsed sacred missions. Each diocese was instructed to have its missionaries, secular or religious and, if the pastor did not engage them, they were to be sent by the bishop.

To indicate some of our present problems and also to propose a certain wonderment at their existence, we turn to the *Code of Canon Law,* promulgated in 1917. We find in the *Code* clear statements on the need for canonical mission, the times when sermons must be preached and even prescriptions on the matter to be preached. Anyone who thinks that the regulations of Vatican Council II on preaching are entirely new has not read the *Code of Canon Law.* We would call special attention to Canon 1344, 1, which says: "On Sundays and holy days of obligation throughout the year, it is the proper duty of every pastor to announce the word of God in the customary homily, especially at the Mass where there is wont to be a greater attendance of people." Canon 1345 reads as follows: "It is to be desired that at all the Masses celebrated in churches and public oratories on holy days of obligation (Sundays) in the presence of the people, a short explanation of the gospel or of some portion of Christian doctrine be given." Canon 1347, 1, says: "In sacred sermons should be explained above all else the things which the faithful must believe and do to be saved;" and in No. 2 of the same canon:

> Let the heralds of the divine word abstain from profane or deep themes that are beyond the average grasp of their hearers; let them carry on their ministry of the gospel not in the persuasive words of human wisdom, or in the profane display and finery of empty, calculating eloquence, but in showing forth spirit and power, preaching not themselves but Jesus crucified.

To our mind also comes another document: the *Normae pro Sacra Praedicatione* of the Sacred Consistorial Congregation, published in 1917 to assist bishops in interpreting and carrying out the canons of the *Code* on preaching.

Kerygmatic Preaching

Much confusion has arisen in preaching circles as a result of the use of the word *kerygma.* Priests have been known to go so far as to say that they wanted nothing to do with it. No preacher who knows the meaning of the word as currently used would want to be against it. Some refer to it as a bit of catechetical jargon. The word, as applied to religious instruction, says little of itself. *Kerygma* means any "publicly announced message." Historically, it is a term used in the writings of the Church to refer to that body of essential truths which God meant to be specifically and emphatically proclaimed.

Scripture scholars use the expression "the great themes" of salvation. In the final analysis Christ is the *kerygma*. He is the good news, the gift of the Father to us. Thus when the Council calls for a "proclamation of God's wonderful works in the history of salvation, the mystery of Christ" (*Const. on Lit.*, No. 35, 2), it is asking for kerygmatic preaching, if you want to call it that!

Reform in the Code of Canon Law

It is well known that Vatican II has set up a post-conciliar commission on the *Code of Canon Law*. The work of this commission will probably take years to accomplish. We do know that the American bishops have asked the Canon Law Society to draft suggestions for reform and the Catholic Homiletic Society was asked to set up a committee to suggest changes and reforms in the canons on preaching. The committee under the chairmanship of Father James McVann C.S.P., J.C.D., has submitted suggestions and some of them have been printed in the current Newsletter of the Society. It is our presumption that similar committees have been set up and suggestions are forthcoming from bodies of territorial bishops in the rest of the world.

Need for Adequate Instruction

It is to be expected that the post-conciliar commission on the reform of the *Code* and the commission of similar nature on the liturgy will be concerned about the problem of adequate instruction of the faithful. That this should be a concern of pope, council, bishop, priest and layman is natural. It is to be hoped, then, that the promise of a greater cycle of Mass formularies with a greater portion of the Scriptures read over a period of years will become a reality. Through the Sunday pericopes and Mass formularies the principal doctrines of the Church and the great salvation themes will be proclaimed to the people with regularity. The preacher, however, must not forget that his homily must also be applied to the life situation of his hearers, that he must bear in mind the principle of liturgical unity and that the *kerygmatic* approach (or whatever he wants to call it) must be adopted in order to proclaim the wonderful works of God in man's salvation.

The Scope of Preaching

Because current emphasis is being placed on the homiletic form, many preachers are concerned about the place of other forms of preaching. The priest is the minister of the word in general as well as in a liturgical sense. The priest is to engage in all forms of preaching, be it at Mass, novenas, devotions, holy hours, retreats, days of recollection, tridua, missions, etc. He is still required to give instructions, to conduct inquiry classes, to teach through the Confraternity of Christian Doctrine, to prepare his people for marriage (the present *Code* calls for a sermon on marriage during Advent and Lent), and to give spiritual guidance in the confessional and at other times.

In a liturgical sense he must be prepared to give the homily at Mass on Sundays and days of precept and at other Masses on days recommended by the decree. The bishop is required to give a homily on the occasion of confirmation, and on the occasion of matrimony the homily must be given. While not required, a homily on the occasion of baptism seems appropriate. The *Constitution on the Liturgy* also calls for the introduction and development of "Bible Services" (cf. *Constitution,* No. 35, 4). Priests have been heard to object to Bible Services on the grounds that they are "too Protestant," "we are down-grading the Rosary", "we are introducing into public worship things that should remain private," etc.

Let all of us try to understand the religious changes that have been sweeping the world for some time, the rise in the educational level of all people, the desire of the Church for Christian unity. The introduction of and emphasis on new forms of liturgical worship is not to "do away" with others but to develop in our people a closer attachment to the word of God.

At this moment it might be well to clarify a statement heard recently that bishops in some parts of the world are granting faculties to the laity to preach. Under present legislation I doubt that this is true, but it may stem from a section of the *Instruction on the Liturgy* of the Post-Conciliar Commission and the Sacred Congregation of Rites, paragraph 37:

> In places which lack a priest, if no priest is available for the celebration of Mass on Sundays and feast days of precept, the sacred celebration of the word of God shall be fostered, according to the judgment of the local Ordinary, with a deacon or even a layman, authorized for this purpose, presiding over the service. The pattern of this celebration shall be almost the same as the liturgy of the word in Mass; ordinarily the epistle and gospel of the Mass of the day shall be read in the vernacular, with chants, especially from the psalms, before the lessons and between them; the one who presides shall give a homily, if he is a deacon; if not a deacon, he shall read a homily indicated by the bishop or the pastor; and the whole celebration shall be closed with the "common prayer" or "prayer of the faithful" and with the Lord's prayer.

Some confusion has been noted on the times that homilies *must* or *may* be given. A reading of paragraphs 53, 54 and 55 of the Postconciliar *Instruction* may be in order:

> 53. There *shall be* a homily on *Sundays* and *feast days of precept* in all Masses which are celebrated *with the people* present.

No exception may be made for conventual, sung, or pontifical Masses.

On *other* days, a homily is *recommended*, especially on *some* of the weekdays of Advent and Lent, as well as in other circumstances when the people come to church in larger numbers.

54. By a homily from the sacred text is understood an explanation either of some aspect of the readings from Holy Scripture or of another text from the Ordinary or Proper of the Mass of the day, taking into account the mystery which is being celebrated and the particular needs of the hearers.

55. If *plans of preaching within Mass* are proposed for *certain periods*, the intimate connection with at least the principal seasons and feasts of the liturgical year (cf. *Const.*, Art. 102-104), that is, with the mystery of the Redemption, is to be harmoniously preserved: for the homily is part of the liturgy of the day.

Problems of Time

There are many other problems with his preaching that confront the priest, especially the one engaged in the parish ministry. There is the question of the time allotted for each Sunday Mass, the lengthening of the service by the use of processions, hymn-singing, an increase in the numbers receiving Holy Communion, the size of the parking lot and the traffic difficulties near the church, the lack of adequate time in a busy, active schedule to prepare the homily properly. It is our ardent hope that most of these will be solved by scheduling Masses over a greater portion of Sundays and days of precept, which seems to be the present trend in the Church. In some parts of the world permission has already been granted to fulfill the Sunday obligation on either Saturday or Sunday. It is also our prayer that the great emphasis placed on preaching by the Council will cause all of us to put the homily high on the list of duties to be fulfilled.

Bibliography

Before concluding we would like to call your attention to the bibliography. It is hardly exhaustive but we tried to keep in mind the needs of all as well as reasonable limitations. On the list you will find books that go deep into a study of the liturgy and theology of preaching and you will find articles and even pamphlets for the busy priest, who wants to get at least a short, adequate grasp of essentials. Because the priest must do a great deal of oral reading we have suggested a book that orients itself around religious materials and experience, which while not ex-professo Catholic can be easily adapted to the Catholic ministry.

CONCLUSION

In conclusion we may say that the Sunday and Holyday homily may take its material and some of its form from: the Mass formulary of the day, the Ordinary of the Mass, Scripture in general, liturgy in general, assigned topics (related as much as possible to the liturgy of the day or the season), and it should be related in some way to the Eucharistic action to follow. Mass should not be used just as an occasion for preaching, e.g. dedicating a library, an organ etc.; a Bible service would be more appropriate.

The priest becomes a herald of the glorious message of salvation, a prophet, chosen by God, sanctified and given his canonical mission (sent) by the Church. He is the principal minister in the liturgy of the word and the liturgy of the Eucharist. It would be hoped that the word might become flesh in the preacher; that he might reveal God yet reflect humanity. Since he cannot be a person independently of people, he must relate himself and his message not to the vague notion of 'congregation' but to the individual personality. In this way he will be fulfilling in his own life, in the portion of the vineyard assigned to him at this moment, the command of the Lord: "Go into the whole world and preach the Gospel to every creature."

BIBLIOGRAPHY

Barth, Karl. *The Preaching of the Gospel.* Philadelphia: Westminster Press, 1963.

Baum, Gregory, O.S.A. *Word and Sacraments in the Church.*

Brack. *Effective Oral Interpretation for Religious Leaders.* Englewood Cliffs: Prentice Hall.

Catholic Homiletic Society. *Newsletter*—Techny, Illinois (Active membership, $10.00 per yr.; associate, $5.00.).

Canisianum. *The Word—Readings in Theology.* Innsbruck: P. J. Kennedy and Sons, 1964.

Connors, Joseph M., S.V.D. *Science of the Sunday Sermon.* Techny: Catholic Homiletic Society.

Drury, Ronan, editor, *Preaching.* New York: Sheed and Ward, 1962.

Haring, Bernard, C.SS.R. *God's Word and Man's Response.* Paulist Press.

Hitz, Paul. *To Preach the Gospel.* New York: Sheed and Ward, 1963.

Hofinger, Johannes. *The ABC's of Modern Catechetics.* Chicago: W. H. Sadlier, 1962.

Jungmann, Josef, S.J. *The Good News Yesterday and Today.* Chicago: Sadlier, 1962.

Liturgical Conference. *Proceedings, 1964.* Washington, D.C.

Murphy-O'Connor, Jerome, O.P. *Paul on Preaching.* New York: Sheed and Ward, 1963.

Priest, The. (October, 1964).

Semmelroth, Otto. *The Preaching Word.* Herder and Herder, 1965.

Sloyan, Gerard S., and McManus, Frederick R. *Priest's Guide to Parish Worship.* Washington: Liturgical Conference.

Worship. (January, March 1964).

THE SACRED SCRIPTURES AND PREACHING

by

Reverend Richard Kugelman, C.P.

Preaching belongs to the "salvation history." It is an essential element of the present phase of salvation history, of "these last days," the period between the Lord's Exaltation and the Parousia. The last verse of Mark's gospel tells us that the risen Lord commanded the apostles to go into the whole world and preach the gospel to every creature. On Pentecost the exalted Lord sent the promised Spirit to His Church to empower her to fulfill this mission, to enable her to bear witness to Him in Jerusalem and Judea, in Samaria and to the ends of the earth (Acts 1:8). Ever since that day, when Peter lifted up his voice and made the bold proclamation: "let all the house of Israel therefore know assuredly that God has made him both Lord and Christ, this Jesus whom you crucified" (Acts 2:36), the Church, through the power of the indwelling Spirit, has been witnessing to her Lord, preaching the good news of salvation in Jesus.

Preaching in the Church today is the continuation of apostolic preaching. Even as the apostles, the priest is commissioned by Christ and empowered by the Spirit to proclaim to the world that Jesus Christ is Lord and Savior. He is not sent to teach a philosophy but to proclaim facts; namely, that Jesus Christ, God's Incarnate Son, has accomplished mankind's salvation in His death and resurrection and that He reigns now, dispensing that salvation in His Church until the end of time when He will return in glory to complete His victory in the Parousia and the glorious Resurrection of the just. Christ is the Word of God, the creative Word through whom all things were made; He is the Word which revealed God's wisdom to Israel in the Torah;

He is the power of God; in Him God accomplished the salvation promised and prepared for in the Old Covenant. In Him God, "Who in many and various ways spoke of old to our fathers by the prophets" (Heb 1:1) reveals Himself. He "who is in the bosom of the Father, has made him known" (Jn 1:18).

Preaching is an essential factor in the process of salvation because God, in that divine foolishness, which is wiser than men, has ordained that men should come to know Him in Christ and should be called to salvation in Christ through the word of a preacher. "How are men to call upon him in whom they have not believed? And how are they to believe in him of whom they have never heard? And how are they to hear without a preacher?" (Rom 10:14).

The apostles have shown the priest how he should preach Christ. Because Jesus is God's Word Incarnate, the apostles continually had recourse in their preaching to the deeds and sayings of Jesus through which He was revealing God, and to the Old Testament Scriptures, which are God's written word, the divinely inspired record of God's actions and promises for mankind's salvation in Israel's history.

For the apostles, to preach the gospel meant to preach Jesus of Nazareth, dead and risen, as the goal of the historical process of the Old Testament and the fulfillment of its promises. The entire New Testament—gospels and Acts, epistles and Apocalypse—illustrates this.

When we come to New Testament Scriptures the relation between the Church's preaching and the inspired word of God is even more intimate. The gospels are rooted in and are the record of apostolic preaching. Many of the forms, or units, of which the synoptic gospels are composed originated in apostolic preaching. The gospel pericopes frequently reflect a Christian preacher's use of the deeds and sayings of Jesus to meet the needs or to solve the problems of the primitive Church. In the fourth gospel we have the mature fruit of the beloved disciple's lifelong meditation and preaching on the mystery of the person of Jesus and on the mystery of His continued presence and saving activity in the Church.

Since the theme of the Church's preaching is Christ, "the end of the law unto justification for every one who believes" (Rom 10:4), i.e., the goal and fulfillment of the salvation history of the Old Testament, and since the New Testament is an inspired record of the apostolic preaching, it follows that the preaching of the priest should be Biblical. The written word of God as understood, interpreted and taught by the Church, whom the indwelling Spirit is guiding into an ever deeper knowledge of the mystery of Christ, should be the source of Catholic preaching. The liturgical texts and the patristic sermons show the Church's keen awareness of this.

The vocation and mission of the preacher is to break the bread of God's word for the men of his day; to proclaim and apply the Biblical message to his audience. Preaching, consequently, should always be an exposition of Sacred Scripture. C. K. Barret, the English Methodist New Testament scholar, expressed this nicely in a lecture on "Biblical Preaching and Biblical Scholarship":

> There is one Word of God—Jesus Christ, the Son of God, who was incarnate, suffered under Pontius Pilate, and rose from the dead. It is through this Word—who Himself is God—that God is known to us as the merciful and redeeming Lord. We know this divine Word through the testimony borne to him by prophets and apostles, borne in the first place through their spoken words, and then transferred to paper and ink, in Scripture. This scriptural witness to the eternal Word is the only valid starting-point for preaching, which *formally* therefore is exposition.[1]

He goes on to declare that you can no more have a Christian sermon without an exposition of the inspired word of God than you can have baptism without water, or the Eucharist without bread and wine. This, I think, is also clearly implied in the Apostle's precepts to Timothy:

> Attend to the public reading of scripture, to preaching, to teaching (I Tim 4:13). All scripture is inspired by God and profitable for teaching, for reproof, for correction, and for training in righteousness that the man of God may be complete, equipped for every good work (2 Tim 3:16); I charge you in the presence of God and of Christ Jesus who is to judge the living and the dead, and by his appearing and his kingdom; preach the word, be urgent in season and out of season, convince, rebuke, and exhort, be unfailing in patience and teaching (2 Tim 4:1-2).

There is an intimate relation between preaching and exegesis. Because preaching is an exposition of the Scriptures as read and understood in the Church, the work of Catholic exegesis is fundamental to preaching. But the two are not identical. The Biblical exposition of the preacher presupposes and uses the work of the exegete, but it goes beyond exegesis. The task of the Catholic exegete is, first of all, that of any scientific exegete, no matter what his faith or lack of faith; namely, to discover the meaning intended by the human author of the passage under consideration. In order to recapture this meaning the exegete must avail himself of all the resources at hand which will enable him to reconstruct the text, its historical context, the idiom, the thought patterns, the literary form of the writer. Then, because he knows by faith that the book he is studying has been inspired by the one divine Spirit who inspired all the canonical Scriptures, and who leads the Church into an ever deeper understanding of them, the Catholic exegete must locate the passage under study in its proper place in the developing process of salvation history; he must consider its use, if any, in later inspired writings and finally by the teaching Church. Thus, in order to discover the full meaning intended by God in the inspired Scripture, the exegete becomes a theologian.

The preacher begins where the exegete-theologian leaves off. Guided by the Catholic Biblical scholar's work, the preacher expounds the Scriptures to the living audience before him, pointing out its timeliness and its relevance to his listener's needs and problems.

Textual criticism, historical criticism and literary criticism are the business of the exegete. It is the business of the Catholic exegete to elucidate the divine meaning of the Biblical event or teaching as part of a progressive revelation and an historical process which culminated in Christ and his Church. It is the preacher's business to expound and apply the Biblical message to the men of today. C. K. Barrett says this very well:

> Scholarship waits upon preaching as its handmaid. Preaching is a vital and indispensable activity of the Church, and scholarship must assist it, not dominate it. Much of the apparatus of scholarship should never appear in the pulpit at all . . . preachers are not called upon to amuse their hearers with tales of the hypothetical Q and the rest of the critical alphabet. It is the Church's business to preach, and it is the scholar's business not to get in the way of this preaching, but rather to assist it as far as he can.[2]

The people to whom we preach are like people everywhere, or all times; they think with their imagination and emotions. The word of God expressed in the Scriptures is often clothed in metaphors which lack meaning and color for a twentieth century Western mind. The preacher learns from the scholar the exact meaning of the Biblical language, but he has the task of translating this into language that will be so meaningful it will move a modern American to give himself ever more completely to Christ.

While preaching is formally an exposition of the word of God, it is not exclusively exposition. In fact, exposition, in itself, is not preaching. The preacher is a teacher, but not only a teacher. He shares in and continues the prophetic office of Christ. Through the preacher Christ addresses His word to the audience, communicating Himself, asking and eliciting a response. Everytime the priest ascends the pulpit God addresses to him the words He spoke to Jeremiah: "See I place my words in your mouth" (Jr 1:9).

> But do you gird your loins; stand up and tell them all that I command you. Be not crushed on their account, as though I would leave you crushed before them, for it is I this day who have made you a fortified city, a pillar of iron, a wall of brass, against the whole land (Jr 1:17-18).

Confident in God's help, the preacher must expound, exhort, inspire and elicit the response of faith, hope and love. He will fire the imagination of his hearers, touch their hearts and move their wills only if he knows the message of Scripture and expresses it in language meaningful and colorful to his audience.

Scripture itself shows the priest how he should preach the word of God. Let us look at the gospels. At the origin of the gospels stands the apostolic preaching. This preaching of the apostles, like all good preaching, was in immediate contact with its audience. The apostles had lived in close association with Jesus during the public ministry. If they wanted, they could have pooled together their memories and supplied future generations of Christians with all the material and information necessary to compose a history of Jesus' ministry. But they were preachers; so they drew from the storehouse of their memories those events and sayings of Jesus that were relevant to the purpose of their preaching and the needs of the people they were addressing. When preaching to the Jews they insisted on the role of the passion and death of Jesus in the divine plan of salvation, pointing up the veiled allusions of the Old Testament to this mystery. Thus they tried to remove the great stumbling block to the Jews commitment to Christ. Jesus, suffering and dying, is the mysterious Servant of the Lord described in Deutero-Isaiah! Addressing themselves to converts from Judiasm the apostles were careful to show how Jesus fulfills the Old Testament promises. Collections of Old Testament passages for the use of preachers,—"testimonies," to use the term of the Biblical Commission's Instruction of last April on the historicity of the gospels—were compiled very early in the Church's life. For example, both Peter in his Pentecost sermon, and Paul in his sermon in the synagogue of Pisidian Antioch, draw the very same argument for the Resurrection of Jesus from Psalm 15.[3]

When the faithful assembled for the liturgy the apostles would recount the sayings of Jesus that referred to the worship of the Father and to the Christian sacraments; they would tell of those events and acts of Jesus' life which were being recalled in the celebration of the mysteries and which pointed to and illustrated the Lord's saving activity in the sacraments. Perplexing problems arose in the community, e.g., questions about divorce, Jewish observances, the Christian attitude toward gentiles. The apostles settled these problems by recalling the Masters' teaching. By this use of Jesus' sayings and deeds to meet the needs of the community the apostles gave their expression a characteristic form and put them in a context which very often was independent of the actual historical circumstances in which they happened. The evangelists took this material already formed by the preaching Church and used it to compose the written gospels. Each was writing for a particular Church or a group of Churches and with a personal purpose. Each has left the stamp of his own individuality and of his personal theological insights and purpose on his gospel.

The Instruction of April 1964 of the Biblical Commission describes this use of the gospel material by the evangelists:

> The sacred authors for the benefit of the churches, took the earliest body of instruction, which had been handed on orally at first and then in writing—for many soon set their hands to drawing up a narrative of matters concerning the Lord Jesus—and set it down in the four Gospels. In doing this each of them followed a method suitable to the special purpose which he had in view. They selected certain things out of the many which had been handed on; some they synthesized, some they explained with an eye to the situation of the churches.[4]

A comparison of some of the Lord's sayings common to Matthew and Luke will serve to illustrate this. The Our Father is recorded in Matthew 6:7-13 and Luke 11:1-4. In Matthew the *Pater* forms part of the Sermon on the Mount and illustrates Christian prayer in contrast to the prayers of pharisees and gentiles. In Luke it is Jesus' response to the disciples' request: "Lord teach us to pray." The disciples, Luke tells us, had been observing Jesus as he prayed. Note, too, the different wording of the prayer. Matthew's longer formula is probably due to additions made in the liturgical use of the prayer in the Churches of Syria.[4] Probably in its original form as taught by Christ and recited by the apostles during the ministry of Jesus the petition, "thy kingdom come," was intended by Our Lord as a prayer for the accomplishment of His mission and His glorification through His Passion, Death and Resurrection. Recited by the primitive Christians after Pentecost it was probably a petition for the Parousia. In Matthew it becomes a prayer for the fulfillment of God's will here by Christian fidelity. "Thy will be done on earth as it is in heaven."

Matthew 18:12-14 and Luke 15:1-7 record the parable of the Lost Sheep. Matthew places the parable in the ecclesiastical discourse of his fifth booklet and draws from it a lesson for the conduct of the authorities of the Church. He introduces it with this saying of Jesus: "See that you do not despise one of these little ones; for I tell you that in heaven their angels always behold the face of my Father who is in heaven" (Mt 18:10). He concludes the parable with another saying: "So it is not the will of my Father who is in heaven that one of these little ones should perish" (Mt 18:14). The shepherd's concern for the lost sheep illustrates the care and concern the authorities of the Church should have for the little ones, the weak and lowly of Christ's flock.

In Luke the parable is the first of a trilogy (lost sheep, lost coin, prodigal son) all of which illustrate Jesus' love for sinners and the joy of God and heaven over the sinner's conversion. Luke tells us: "Now the tax collectors and sinners were all drawing near to hear him. And the pharisees and scribes murmured, saying, 'This man receives sinners and eats with them.'" Our Blessed Lord told the parable to illustrate his love for sinners and zeal for their salvation. The first preachers probably used the parable to justify, in face of Jewish-Christian opposition, the mission to the gentiles and their admission to the community. The evangelist Luke probably narrates it to exhort the faithful to be zealous for the conversion of their sinful Christian brothers and to receive the repentant with joyful love.

Note how both Matthew and Luke are not simply exegeting the sayings and parable of Jesus; they point out the relevance of Jesus' words, their lesson for the Christians for whom they wrote their respective gospels. But note, too, how the evangelists never betray, never distort or falsify the meaning of Jesus; they always preserve the basic meaning of Jesus' words, although in applying them to their audience and adapting them to their particular purposes, they bring out different nuances.

The preacher, if he is to avoid distorting the meaning of Scripture, must consult the exegetes. But as a preacher he is always addressing a particular audience. He must always keep before him the particular needs and circumstances of his audience and the purpose he has in preaching to them. He must use the New Testament relevantly. There are good precedents for this practice—the apostolic preaching, the evangelists, the Church's liturgy. With reference to the liturgy, the preacher of the homily usually finds the lesson he should draw from the Scripture readings indicated for him by the use the liturgy of the day is making of them. He must expound this word of God, not precisely as it is presented in the sacred book from which it has been taken, but according to the liturgical context in which the Church has placed it. The Church has followed in her liturgical use of Scripture readings the example of the apostles and the evangelists in their narration of Jeseus' deeds and sayings. A knowledge of the history of the Mass texts will help the preacher understand the particular lessons the Church intends in the scripture readings of the Masses of the liturgical seasons.

For example, one must know something about the practices of the ancient catechumenate and about the ancient penitential discipline to understand the choice of the Scripture readings of the Lenten Masses. Such knowledge is indispensable in order to expound the Scriptures as read in the liturgy. But the preacher should not give a historical discourse on the ancient practices of the Church. The Scripture readings of this Mass, intended originally for the catechumens or public penitents of the ancient Church are read today to a congregation which contains no catechumens and no public penitents but which is made up of the baptized and of sinners. The preacher fails unless he shows the relevance of the Biblical message in this liturgical context for his present, living audience.

Now let us turn to the preacher's use of the Old Testament. Here, again, Scripture and the liturgy show the way to the preacher. Like the New Testament authors and the liturgy the preacher should read the Old Testament by the light of Christian faith by which he knows that Christ and his Church are the goal of the Old Testament history and the fulfillment of its hopes and promises. The Old Testament without the new is like a mystery story with the last chapter torn out. We Christians have the last chapter and know its contents. So we can recognize the clues scattered throughout the earlier chapters and see the denouement toward which they converge. For example, without the New Testament and Christian faith it would be very difficult not to conclude from the prophets and royal psalms that the Messiah would be a powerful political leader, a glorious monarch of a prosperous and victorious kingdom of this world. It is true that there are the mysterious Servant poems of Deutero-Isaiah; but never in the Old Testament do the two lines, royal messianism and suffering servant, converge.

The Christian preacher must read the Old Testament by the light of his faith, and, like the risen Lord for the two disciples on the road to Emmaus, he must, beginning with Moses and all the prophets interpret for his audience in all the Scriptures the things concerning Christ.[5]

The New Testament writers more frequently use the Old Testament according to "the fuller sense" and the "typical sense," than according to the historical or primary literal sense. Christian faith illumines the record of God's saving acts in Israel's history and the oracles of her prophets, so that the inspired Old Testament says more to the believing Christian than was comprehended by its first readers and even by its human authors.

The term "fuller sense," *sensus plenior,* is modern, having been coined in the late Twenties by the late Father Fernandez of the Biblical Institute. The nature of this sense of Scripture is controverted. Some even deny it any existence distinct from what has been called the spiritual or typical sense. Should it be placed under the literal sense, or is it simply the typical sense? But of this fact there can be no question, no matter what terminology one uses to designate it, the New Testament authors do frequently, almost always, draw from the words of the Old Testament a deeper meaning, a fuller meaning, a Christian meaning, which the human authors did not perceive at all, or at most, only obscurely. With Pere Benoit, O.P., I would place this fuller sense under the literal sense as a meaning of Scripture really intended by God, provided it is restricted to the fuller meaning of a Biblical text given by a later Biblical book. I would like to cite Pere Benoit:

> Only faith knows that the same divine author has written the Law and the Prophets, the Epistles and the Gospels, and can therefore have established among them mysterious harmonies.

. . . The normal, the habitual manner for a Christian to understand the Old Testament is according to the fuller sense. It has
been asked if the citations of the Old Testament in the New
Testament do not at times arrive at a fuller sense. Why, that is
what they usually give! If the New Testament does occupy itself
with the ancient historical meaning, it is only to oppose to it the
Christian transposition which gives its fuller meaning; thus the
antitheses of the Sermon on the Mount. And the same must be
said of the ancient Fathers; their exegesis is usually theological
and it is the fuller meaning which they draw out of the texts.[6]

The New Testament application to Christ of Nathan's promise to
David: "I will raise up your offspring after you, who shall come
forth from your body, and I will establish the throne of his kingdom
forever" (2 Sm 7:12-13) is, I submit, the perception of a fuller
meaning than intended by the prophet and understood by David.
Nathan was referring to David's heir, Solomon; Luke 1:32 sees
the oracle fully realized in Mary's child. The Johannine allusions
to Genesis 3:15 in Chapter 12 of the Apocalypse and in John 19:26
draw out of the ancient protoevangelium a Christian meaning, a fuller
meaning never suspected by the Yahwist collector of Israel's traditions or by the priest editors of Genesis. The New Testament application of the Royal Psalms to Christ gives a fuller Christian meaning
of the ancient hymns—a meaning intended indeed by God the principal author but not perceived by his instrument, the human author.
I think we can trace, at times, in the Bible the unfolding of this
fuller sense.

For example, Psalm 2, the great Messianic Psalm, which contains
the divine declaration to Israel's king: "You are my son; this day I
have begotten you." Originally the Psalm was sung at the enthronement of a king of Juda on whose lips the singer places Nathan's
oracle to David in which God promises to regard and treat as a son
the kings of the Davidic dynasty. "I will be his father and he shall
be my son" (2 Sm 7:14). Understood thus the Psalm is typically
messianic, in as much as the kings of Juda prefigure the great Son
of David to come. But Psalm 2 has come to us in the psalter of post-
exilic Judaism. Sung at Israel's worship, when God's people no longer
had a king of David's line, the psalm expressed Israel's faith and hope
for the promised Messiah king. On the day of the Messiah's mani-
festation God would confirm for him the promise of the Davidic
covenant: "You are my son; this day I have begotten you." In this
post-exilic psalter the song is literally messianic.

We come now to the New Testament. St. Paul sees the oracle fulfilled in Jesus' resurrection; this is the enthronement of Christ; it is
then he receives the title Lord and begins his messianic reign.[7] The
author of Hebrews 1:5, "For to what angel did God ever say, 'Thou
art my Son, today I have begotten thee?'," probably also applies the
Psalm text to Our Lord's resurrection, or he may, possibly, be refer-

ring it to the Incarnation as Luke 1:35, understands it. The synoptic tradition sees this decree of God promulgated at the Baptism.[8] All these New Testament passages draw from the Psalm a fuller, Christian meaning.

When not interpreting the Old Testament according to a fuller sense, the New Testament authors usually read it as the record of God's saving acts which not only prepared for and led to Christ and his Church, but which also, by the divine will, foreshadowed and typified the New Covenant. This is especially true of the Exodus story. Paul sees Christian baptism prefigured in the passage through the sea; John sees the Eucharist prefigured in the manna, and the Lord's gift of the Spirit in the water struck from the rock by Moses. For Matthew, Jesus is the new and greater Moses promulgating the new law on a new mountain. Speaking of this history of Israel during the period of the wandering, Paul tells the Corinthians: "Now these things were written down for our instruction upon whom the end of the ages has come" (1 Cor 10:11). You are all very familiar with this typological use of the Old Testament not only in the New Testament, but especially in the liturgy and the fathers.

The typology of the Exodus in the New Testament and the liturgy is intimately related with the development of a theological theme enunciated in the literal sense of the Scriptures. There is a harmony between the two covenants, between the religious truths which Old Testament faith saw in the Exodus events and the Christian realities which New Testament faith sees typified in them. This real harmony between the two covenants was willed by God and is the basis of typology. The events, persons and things of the Old Testament are figurative of New Testament realities when they occupy in the Old Covenant positions analagous to those held by the corresponding realities in the New Covenant. Typology, I think, is much more extensive than many are ready to admit. But its use must be cautious and restrained, lest it fall into the old Philonian abuse of the Scriptures, into a fantastic allegorism. Usually the preacher should keep to the types employed by the New Testament, the liturgy and the Fathers. We are certain of the typical meaning of a Biblical passage only when it has been explained typically in a later Biblical book, or when the Church has clearly indicated the typology, e.g., in her liturgical use of the Old Testament. The preacher will find Père Danielou's studies in the Biblical Typology of the Fathers, *From Shadows to Reality* instructive and useful. He concludes: "We meet an agreement of all schools upon the fundamental types. This proves that we are face to face with something which is part and parcel of the deposit of Revelation." [9] I submit that the preacher who relates the Christian mysteries, e.g., the sacraments, to their Old Testament types will preach sermons that will be instructive, interesting and colorful. He will also, without even adverting to it, be driving home to his audience the basic truth of the relationship of Christianity to the Old Testament Covenant and he will arouse interest in the Old Testament and the desire to know more about it.

I would like now to express in some practical propositions what I think are the conclusions to be drawn from my paper.

1) Ordinarily we should not preach simply on an isolated text of Sacred Scripture, but rather (a) on the great Biblical themes developed in the Scriptures and (b) on the religious teaching of selected Biblical pericopes.

2) Our sermon preparation should begin with the reading of Scripture. All too frequently, I fear, preachers compose their sermons and then thumb through the concordance to find texts with which to pad it. This leads, at times, to putting on the text a meaning never intended in any way by the Holy Spirit; at other times, it gives the sermon the appearance of a cento of citations, which robs the sermon of spontaneity and can be very wearing on the audience.

3) We should clothe the message of the Biblical passages we are expounding in language that is meaningful and colorful to a twentieth century American audience.

4) Following the example of the New Testament authors, especially of the gospels, we should apply the deeds and sayings of Jesus to our particular audience and relevantly to our particular purpose, being careful always not to distort the basic meaning of the inspired text.

5) Again, following the lead of the New Testament, the liturgy and the fathers, we should usually employ the Old Testament according to its fuller, Christian meaning or in its typological meaning.

The preacher who presents the message of the Scriptures in this way will enlighten, inspire and move his audience. With the disciples at Emmaus they will say: "Did not our hearts burn within us while he talked to us, . . . while he opened to us the scriptures" (Lk 24:32).

FOOTNOTES

[1] C. K. Barrett, *Biblical Problems and Biblical Preaching* (Fortress Press, Philadelphia, 1964) p. 29.

[2] *Ibid.*

[3] *Acts* 2:24-31; 13:34-37.

[4] Cf. the *Didache* 8.

[5] *Luke* 24:27.

[6] P. 192f P. Benoit, O.P., *La plenitude de sens des Livres Saints,* RB 67, 1960, 161-196.

[7] *Acts* 13:33; *Rom.* 1:4.

[8] *Mark* 1:11.

[9] Jean Danielou, S.J., *From Shadow to Reality,* Studies in the Biblical Typology of the Fathers (The Newman Press, Westminster, Md., 1960), p. 288.

BIBLIOGRAPHY

Ahern, Barnabas M., C.P. "The Scriptures and Preaching," *Proceedings of The Catholic Homiletic Society 1959*, republished in the *Passionist*, Dec. 1962, 265-271.

Assemblees du Seigneur, *Biblica*, Bruges, Belgium.

Barrett, C. K., *Biblical Problems and Biblical Preaching* (Fortress Press, Philadelphia, 1964).

Barrosse, T., C.S.C. "The Senses of Scripture and the Liturgical Pericopes," *C.B.Q.* 21, 1959, 1-23.

Benoit, P., O.P., "La Plenitude de sens des Livres Saints," *Revue biblique*, 67, 1960, 161-196.

Bouyer, Louis, "Liturgie et exegese spirituelle," *La Maison-Dieu*, VII, 1946, 27-50.

Boylan, P., "Scripture and Preaching," in *Preaching* edited by Ronan Drury, pp. 110-119, (Sheed and Ward, New York, 1963).

Brown, Raymond, S.S., *The Sensus Plenoir of Sacred Scripture*, St. Mary's University (Baltimore, 1955).

Burghardt, Walter J., S.J. "On Early Christian Exegesis," *Theological Studies 11*, 1950, 78-116.

Danielou, Jean, S.J., "The Fathers and the Scriptures," *The Eastern Churches Quarterly X*, no. 6, Summer 1954, 265-273.

————. "From Shadow to Reality," *Studies in the Biblical Typology of the Fathers*, (The Newman Press, Westminster, Md., 1960).

Dodd, C. H. "According to the Scriptures," (Scribner, New York, 1953).

————. "The Apostolic Preaching and Its Developments," (Harper & Brothers, New York, 1960).

————. "The Old Testament in the New," (Fortress Press, Philadelphia, 1963).

Fitzmeyer, J. A., S.J. "The Biblical Commission's Instruction on the Historical Truth of the Gospels," *Theological Studies*, 25, 1964, 386-408.

Fuller, Reginald H., "What is Liturgical Preaching," Studies in Ministry and Worship (SCM Press, London, 1957).

Graf, Ernest, O.S.B. "The Bible and The Preacher," *The Homiletic and Pastoral Review*, XLVI, No. 7, April 1946, 517-522.

Guide de l'Assemblee Chretienne (5 vols.) Casterman, 1965.

Kugelman, R., C.P. "Preaching and The Word of God," *The Bible Today*, Oct. 1964, 845-851.

The Liturgy and the Word of God, Mortimer et al. (Liturgical Press, Collegeville, 1959).

Pope John XXIII on Preaching, *The Pope Speaks*, 1959, Spring Vol. 5, No. 2, 275-279; 1960, Summer Vol. 6, No. 3, 49-54.

Semmelroth, O., *Preaching and the Word*, (Herder, St. Louis, 1965).

"The *Sensus Plenior* in the Last Ten Years," *C.B.Q.* 25, 1963, 262-285.

Vawter, Bruce, C.M., "The Fuller Sense, Some Considerations," *C.B.Q.* 26, 1964, 85-96.

Von Allmen, Jean-Jacques, "Preaching and Congregation," translated by B. L. Nicholis, *Ecumenical Studies in Worship*, No. 10, (John Knox Press, Richmond, Va., 1962).

Von Balthasar, U., "Word and Preaching," (Herder, St. Louis, 1964).

Woestelandt, M., *Plan de Predication sur l'Ecriture*, Apostolat liturgique, Bruges, 1958.

The Word, an anthology, (Kenedy, New York, 1964).

PREACHING SALVATION HISTORY

by

Very Reverend Alan Smith, O.P.

If we preach the Sacred Scriptures, we have problems. J. B. Priestley, the English novelist, put one of them vividly when he spoke of how strange and outlandish the Bible seems, given the audience of today. Just picture mild-mannered clerks and hard-fisted truck-drivers, exquisitely gowned ladies and hard-working mothers—all the varied and sundry who listen to the wild oriental imagery, the tales of ancient and terribly savage warfare, the lust and pride of hook-nosed and raven-bearded chieftains, of sacrifice and butchery on the glaring deserts of the Middle East. As Priestley put it, they sing . . .

> in unison their hope of an immortality to be spent in cities built of blazing jewels, where kings played harps and maidens clashed the cymbals; one could not help wondering what these people would do if they really did find themselves billeted for ever in this world of the Eastern religious poets. What had these sober . . . islanders to do with all this Oriental stuff? What did it, what could it really mean to them? Could anything be less aptly shaped and coloured to match their own lives? If this was the time when their thoughts turned to the creator of this universe, when they were asked to consider the deep truths of this life, to face their consciences and search their hearts, why should they be dragged into the far-away fantastic world of goats and vines and smoking sacrifices and tribal kings? . . . Must God . . . remain for ever in Asia? Are these people always to assume that he is still brooding over Babylon? [1]

That is our first problem—one of space and time and mentality or outlook. Since Priestley wrote, this problem has, if anything, grown sharper. Why? Because as Hitz says, the catechumenate of society

has either totally disappeared or become ineffective. What does catechumenate of society mean? Simply this. For centuries infants have
been baptized. They became Christians before any instruction in
Christianity was possible. The Church relied in great part on the
Christian family and the Christian community to form, teach and
protect the faith of the young Christian. This Christian social catechumenate formed what amounted to a "pastoral theology of the
sheepfold." Now this sheepfold is non-existent or not enough. We
find the faith enfeebled, weak, because it is no longer so fostered.
People are not so much openly against the faith as just not interested.
We must attract men to the faith, we must revitalize, renew their faith.[2]

But what attracts the man of today? We can get some inkling from
studying the wiles of the advertising world. They put their best minds
to work on doing just that. We find their appeals are channeled into
three great categories: comfort, security and success. Our initial
prospect doesn't cheer us. Men want all three, in varying proportions,
perhaps, but they want them *now*. What we have to offer still seems
to them "a pie in the sky by and by." What we present now looks
very much like a cross for comfort, fear and trembling for security,
and a morality that dims, if it does not preclude, success.

However, the picture is not all darkness. Comfort, security, success—all of these in the concrete are not ultimate ends. Men actually
will sacrifice all three for love if the love is strong enough. We know
too many examples of self-sacrificing love to delay on the obvious.
Now what we have to present is a love strong enough. The love we
present has made men give up life itself; we call them martyrs, and
we know that the word means "witness." As witnesses, they testify
with their very lives to the strength of their love and faith in God.

That's the first aim: faith. And we can arouse faith by preaching—
if we have faith.

> For seeing that in the wisdom of God the world, by wisdom,
> knew not God, it pleased God by the foolishness of our preach-
> ing to save them that believe . . . we preach Christ crucified . . .
> unto them that are called, both Jews and Greeks, Christ the
> power of God and the wisdom of God. For the foolishness of
> God is wiser than men; and the weakness of God is stronger
> than men (I Cor 1:21-28).

Many exegetes of St. Paul maintain that when he first began preaching, he preached a message of power—the Resurrection and the
Second Coming. At the Areopagus he argued in a philosophical manner with the learned of Athens; he used all their splendid rhetorical
devices. Their response was a well-mannered rejection: "We must
hear you again sometime." Paul had been brilliant, dynamic, and he
felt he had fallen flat on his face. He left Athens for Corinth as a
dejected man. Now Corinth—a wide-opened town, Las Vegas with
water, the term "Corinthian girl" synonymous with lustful pleasure—

how could Paul succeed there? His life was a failure. Philippi, Thessalonica, Berea—in all those places he had such high hopes; success was close enough to taste when suddenly . . . persecution, and Paul had to flee.

Then Timothy came with unexpected news. Things were going well at Thessalonica, the faith was blooming. Paul was pleased, surprised. He reflected long and earnestly on the meaning of this. He began to see a tremendous truth: the God Who had emptied Himself, had taken on the form of a servant, had been obedient unto death, (Phil 2:6-8) this God conquered in weakness, not only triumphed over suffering but in suffering. The man who deeply believed in God was not really weak when emptied of his own strength; he was filled with God.

Read St. Paul's First Epistle to the Thessalonians:

> Our gospel was not delivered to you in word only, but in power also, and in the Holy Spirit, and in much fullness, as indeed you know what manner of men we have been among you for your sakes. And you become imitators of us and of the Lord, receiving the word *in great tribulation* (I Thess 1:4-7).

It is the theme of the remnant all over again. "The Lord . . . shall again reclaim the remnant of his people" (Is 11:11). The Cross is the seed of the Resurrection; suffering, the seed of glory. This is our message. It is a message of faith calling unto faith.

Obviously, then, the primary call is not for an apologetics of the faith. Apologetics has its place, but the urgent need now does not seem to be rational proofs and clever answers. The motives of credibility are a preparation for the faith, not the faith itself; they are external to it. The best apologetics now seems to be telling what God has done for us in Jesus Christ. When a man hears God's call and believes, it is always because, through the preaching of the Church and the interior movement of the Holy Spirit, the living God calls him to be saved through Christ in the Holy Spirit. Our preaching should put man in the presence of God.

But what kind of preaching? Not simply apologetical, we say, which provides preliminaries, whose end is human credibility. Moral preaching then? No, not that either. This is what gives the average man the notion that Christianity is simply a kill-joy religion, a burden, a religious strait-jacket. That is how the rules of morality look to a feeble faith. Man wants a vision, a loving, joyful vision, to stir him to action. Not a vision that down-grades the obstacles, but one which stirs up the love to overcome them. The boy in love with a girl sees the obstacles, but love moves him to overcome them because they stand in the way of someone he loves. We want to get people in love with God. We have to present a vision—the faith. In a sense we are back to the days of the apostles. We have to arouse the faith. With

faith men see morality as a springboard of action, a minimal require-
ment, an obstacle cut down to size by love of God and God's love in us.

This is an important point—God's love. God has first loved us. Our
love does not mean awakening a response in God; rather our love
depends on God's love for us. We have the assurance in revelation
that God has always taken this initiative of love. In fact, revelation
itself is the expression of God's love, for it is movement of God
towards man. We can find this revelation in the inspired word—in
the history of our salvation.

Preaching salvation history means preaching Christ. It means
preaching that all history leads up to Christ; it means that all history
since that central event—Christ—makes sense only in the light of His
coming. The Christ we believe in is a living Christ, for if Christ be
not risen, our faith is in vain. The Christ we preach is a living Christ;
we are not just talking about what happened two thousand years ago;
we are concerned with Christ Who here and now lives in us and we
in Him. Too good to be true? We can make the classic retort; too
good not to be true and we know it is true by faith.

We have, in the words of St. Leo the Great, to make Christians
conscious of their dignity. In this fantastic world of ours with space
walking and atom splitting, the most fantastic fact is that God the
Father has called us to be His adopted sons, that He has invited us
to share His divine life. "I have come so that they may have life and
have it more abundantly" (Jn 10:10).

How did God tell us this? He acted in history. God's interventions
are always meaningful though their meanings were not always immediately evident. The record of those interventions is in the Bible, and
sometimes the meaning of that record is not always immediately evident either. We must pause to put that record in focus.

We speak of salvation history. The word "history" immediately
springs to the forefront. As Grollenberg has written:

> Belief in their divine origin helped to create the view that the
> Holy Books complied with the (modern) demand for objectivity
> and historical reliability to a far greater degree than any other
> book. The starting point for evaluating Scripture was the idea
> that the various biblical accounts dealt only with historical events
> —with solid, naked facts. . . . Only gradually did the realization
> dawn that this manner of understanding biblical accounts was
> in error.[3]

Modern Biblical studies show us some of the ways in which we must
qualify that word 'historical.' We have been able to some degree to
construct the formation of the Bible. We see that in many books many
strands of tradition, oral and/or written, have been joined, such as
the Yahwist, Elohist, Deuteronomic, Priestly which you undoubtedly
recall in the Pentateuch. The editors who fused or paralleled these
traditions were not always concerned with their lack of harmony.

For example, surely it was noticed way back then that chapters 8 and 12 of the First Book of Kings viewed the institution of the human king in place of Yahweh as sinful, while chapters 9 and 10 considered it a gift of Yahweh Himself. Both views are simply presented without any overt attempt at reconciliation. What kind of history is this?

As Père George points out, and this is an important guideline not only for the Books of Kings but for the gospel as well:

> In their accounts the authors generally wish to affirm real facts. . . . Yet they are often more intent upon the whole than upon details, upon the meaning of the facts rather than upon their material presentation. (This is characteristic of all ancient historians). The sacred author is involved with truth on a higher level, and it is here that he wishes to be heard. On this level he makes no mistake.[4]

Sometimes, too, we may feel uneasy not because of historical inconsistencies or unlikely doublets but simply because the story being told seems bigger than life—Samson, for example. I recall a distinguished professor speaking of Samson's adventures as "tavern tales" which made me wonder—not about Samson, but about the professor. Or we may think of the devastating effects of the plagues of Egypt which seem to be wiping out the same animals and what-not again and again like the Indians in a western. Here once more we must remind ourselves that the Bible is concerned with the religious meaning of the fact and that religious meaning in turn concerns the mystery of the relationship between God and man. It is really a mystery, then, which goes beyond the limits of its appearance as external fact. How is the inspired writer to bring out the intrinsic truth of the external fact? The heightening effect of hyperbole in the saga form of literature was the answer. Meditation upon the event, enlightened of course by the Holy Spirit, revealed its inner meaning and thus unveiled further the divine truth.

Now we have learned to recognize, too, the contributions made by Biblical books which may look like history but are intended predominantly as stories—edifying, consoling, instructing. Books like Jona, Judith, Tobias, Esther, Daniel. We can seek nourishment in their teaching instead of finding uneasiness about their supposed history. They may not be history, but they may not be despised any more than Our Lord's parables. They teach truths useful for salvation.

Even the record contained in the New Testament needs, perhaps, to be put in proper focus. As Schelkle indicates:

> The gospels are not a disinterested objective biography or history of Jesus. They are the proclamation and the demonstration of Jesus as the Christ. The New Testament epistles are not dogmatic treatises; their aim is always to edify and organize the Church by means of the word and by faith. The real aim of the New Testament writings is never therefore just narrative, but always the message. "All that was written," says St. Paul, "was written for

our hope, that through patience and the consolation of the Scriptures we might have edification." [5]

Nor is this just one man's opinion. The recent instruction of the Pontifical Biblical Commission last year sustains this view in part when it speaks of the three levels contained in our gospels: namely, the life of Christ as it was actually lived; secondly, the understanding of Christ in the light of the resurrection by the apostolic church; and thirdly, the redaction of the evangelists whose arrangement and modifications reflect their own inspired theologizing.[6]

Perhaps some brief clarification of this may be useful. The Commission itself gives several examples, one from the second chapter of St. John's gospel. There Christ says: "Destroy this temple, and in three days I will raise it up." At the time those who heard Him thought of the temple literally, but after the resurrection, as St. John tells us, the disciples remembered these words and understood them and believed them as referring to His Body.

In the liturgy of Trinity Sunday, we have another example of the primitive Church's theologizing upon the words of Christ, for in Matthew 28:19 we have the fully developed Trinitarian formula. Yet if our Lord used these actual words of command in the baptismal formula, why do the epistles of St. Paul and the *Acts of the Apostles* speak of being baptized in the name of Jesus only? The Commission's reply enables us to point this out as a later theological explanation, in fact, a climactic one.

A clear example of the evangelists' redactional touches may be seen in the saying of Jesus about taking up the cross. In Matthew 16:24-27, Jesus is speaking to His disciples to take up the cross. In Mark 8:34-38, Jesus is depicted as speaking not only to the disciples but to the *crowd*. And in Luke 9:23-24, Christ's words are addressed to all and have daily application. "Take up his cross daily and follow me."

Some may find this a bit disconcerting, cavalier. It must be stressed, however, that these modifications whether those of the apostolic church or of the evangelist himself are inspired and hence the word of God. Such transformations showed the concern of the early Church to meet definite situations with Christ-inspired solutions and instructions for the faithful. The evangelists are not satisfied with merely teaching what the Master taught; they want this teaching to permeate life. Need I say more to preachers? We can look at such divergencies, then, as the number of beatitudes, the wordings of the "Our Father," or even the exact terminology of the Eucharistic celebration and see a potential source of further enlightment rather than just another problem to be solved.

If we feel dismayed that God should act in this fashion, perhaps we should examine our dismay. Some, for example, are taken aback by the many parallels to Biblical literature in that of ancient surrounding peoples. We have only to think back to the recent past and to recall the reaction of some to the literature of Qumran (Dead Sea Scrolls) and its relations to the New Testament, especially St. John. We are still a bit shocked at God's condescension. We feel His word should really be letters from heaven clearly marked off from everything else by their unhuman origins. The myths of other peoples, for instance, concerning creation or the flood do not really destroy or even taint our Biblical accounts of those events because of similarities. God's word is not being tainted by humanity; on the contrary, man's word has been purified, elevated and transformed by the touch of God. This is a part of the pattern being emphasized by modern Biblical studies. God showing divine empathy for the human situation and not disdaining even to take man-made myths of competing gods and wondrously shaping them into a means of true revelation.

This appreciation of the Biblical approach should lead us to see that our basic relationship is not with the ideas of the text, but rather with the person of God we meet through the imperfect mediation of the text. Through salvation history God more and more reveals Himself to us in a dialogue of love. It is a call to faith and the term of faith is not a proposition but God Himself.

As Derek Lance puts it:

> For the History of Salvation, although it is truly historical, transcends human history. It is not just a record of certain events; it is a dynamic process embracing past, present and future. It is the exciting story of how God has been, and still is, at work in our world, communicating himself to mankind and drawing mankind progressively closer to himself. It is the story of a developing dialogue between God and man; a dialogue between persons.[7]

Salvation history, need we remind you, in practice involves more than Biblical data or a selection of it. Theology as faith seeking understanding must play its role and the liturgy with its power of actualizing the Word of God through the liturgical acts cannot be ignored. As Père Colomb puts it:

> Any narration of an event constitutes a kind of explanation. A theological explanation must in turn rest on revealed data. And these data, plus their theological elaboration, are always present in the liturgical act.[8]

Obviously, the predominance of one of these elements—Bible, theology, liturgy—or the diverse admixture of these will vary according to the end in view.

Perhaps, some general observations may serve as a working framework for considering salvation history as useful to preaching:

(1) Salvation history is concerned with religious values rather than history as such.

(2) The Biblical texts chosen should have an important place in the mystery of the faith.

(3) The text chosen should be interpreted in the light of the faith.

(4) The present value of the past event should be developed.

1. *Salvation history is concerned with religious values rather than history as such.*[9]

What we have already said concerning the Biblical viewpoint of history serves as background here. Père De Vaux wrote in concluding his masterly study of the patriarchs:

> The Bible does not teach us history; it teaches us another lesson—it traces the beginnings of our salvation, the election of Abraham by God, the covenant between God and Abraham . . . the love and care with which God guided and protected this small family because he was already thinking when he called Abraham, of the son of this people who would be His Son and the Redeemer of the world. That which the Bible tells us is a view of the faith which escapes the historian's judgment. But the historian may . . . what we have tried to do . . . regain the historical ground in which these patriarchal traditions are rooted.[10]

What unfolds in the Bible, then, is what St. Paul calls the mystery of Christ, that is, the design of God's love for men revealed in Jesus Christ. Jesus said, "I am the light of the world"; and in His light we read the Biblical books and see not different things, rather we see things differently. We see the unity of history, salvation history, in Christ—the preparation in the Old, the realization in the New, the prolongation in the Church.

The Old Testament was the context of the coming of Christ. As Wilhelm Visher wrote: "The New Testament tells us who Christ is. The Old Testament tells us what Christ is." [11] For Jesus belongs not to an order of human rationality but to the order of the mighty works of God. These almighty works of God constitute a pattern, a pattern of God's love for men.

Further, the Old Testament not only testifies to God's works in the past but heralds His works of the future. What God has done in the past arouses the expectation of what God will do. The basis for this is God's fidelity, His faithfulness to His promises. This expectation, this hope, was fostered by the prophets.

The prophets, those spokesmen of God, established what would be a relationship between the past and the future works of God. As Danielou points out:

> There is a fundamental analogy between these works. The new creation will be a taking-up-again of the first creation, and the new Exodus will be a deliverance like the old. And this means quite simply that, being the work of the same God, they reveal the ways of God, which are the same. By this means the

legitimacy of the comparison between past works and future works is established. This mutual relationship is called typology. It provides a permanent context, an order of things.[12]

The light of Christ illuminates too another prophetic proclamation: that the works God will do (which are actually realized in Christ) will be greater than those of the past. As Isaiah 43: 18-19 writes: "Do not remember those old things, as if you had eyes for nothing but what happened long ago; I mean to perform new wonders." We must remember in reading this what those past events had meant and did mean to Israel. The events of the Exodus had made them a people, a people of God, and when catastrophe struck, they looked back upon it as a pledge of faith in the God Who loved them. Now their eyes are being directed towards a future Messianic age, and we know from the light of Christ that the prophets spoke truly. The creation will be a new creation with Christ the new Adam, the covenant will not be cut in stone—it will be the very Christ, and the deliverance will not be from evil men but from the kingdom of evil. In Jesus Christ we have at one and the same time revelation, that is God moving towards men, and religion, that is man moving towards God.

Christ, then, is the fulfillment, the realization, but the end is not yet. If Christ is the sacrament of God, the Church is the sacrament of Christ and His prolongation, His continuation on earth. And in that Church we have the Spirit of God telling us all truth. This is the milieu of our salvation history—where God acts on us and in us and where we respond in faith and love.

Salvation history thus brings out the religious values of history, for God is the Lord of history. Even man's failures to respond, for God respects man's freedom, do not destroy the over-all design of God for man. St. Augustine saw this so long long ago, and we join him when we too look upon original sin and cry out, "Happy fault."

2. *The Biblical texts chosen should have an important place in salvation history.*

This seems only common sense unless we are seeking to do things the hard way. The texts which have this important bearing are the more likely to be fruitful in development. In practice we can recognize the important themes and the texts bearing on them from the works of skilled exegetes. We have, for example, such thematic treatments as those of Guillet's *Themes of the Bible*, Gilbert's *God of Israel—God of Christians*. Recently, too, we have the two volume source book by Maertens *Biblical Themes*.[13] This contains, among many other things, suggested themes for all the epistles and gospels on Sunday throughout the year, and may be worth your perusal.

Maertens describes a theme briefly and, then, follows with Scriptural references, each reference being also briefly described. For example,

the gospel for the Third Sunday after Pentecost is Luke 15:1-10, the
lost sheep and lost coin. Maertens considers the theme of shepherd.
He traces this theme in the Bible showing that it evoked a nomadic
civilization and a particular status on the social level, but that the
Bible had added to this a religious note, that of a search after God.
He mentions also that the prophets had foreseen two accomplishments,
(a) that God would Himself be the Shepherd; and (b) that the King-
Messias would be the Shepherd, and that these two traditions would
be joined in the person of Jesus, God and Messias at the same time.
Finally, he refers to connected themes such as shepherd and judge;
shepherd and strength; shepherd and unity; etc. This evidently does
not mean pre-written sermons or homilies, but I do think it will give
substance to our Biblical approaches.

Often, too, in connection with important Biblical texts we hear the
word *kerygma,* that essential body of truths which God meant as the
core of our teaching. Many have given summaries of this *kerygma.*
One of the briefer yet complete ones is that of William Reedy.[14] This
is his summary:

> Out of his infinite goodness and love (no merit on our part),
> God the Father has invited us to share with him his own divine
> life through Jesus Christ, whom he gave, a ransom for sinners.
> (Eph. 2, 7; 1 Pet. 5, 10; Jn. 17, 21; Rom. 8, 29)
> Born anew of water and the Spirit we are transformed into
> the likeness of Christ who acts in us by grace so that we, living
> God's life in time in the Church which is Christ, do good works
> under the lawful direction of the superiors he has appointed for
> us. (Rom. 6,3; 1 Jn. 4, 10; 1 Cor. 12, 13; Acts 20, 28)
> As children of God we have been sent the Spirit so that we
> will be enabled to render a service of love and a continuous
> sacrifice of praise to the Father through Christ. Thus we are
> temples of God, truly Christ's body, nourished by Christ's own
> flesh and blood in the new life we are called to live. (Gal. 4,6;
> Heb. 13, 15; Eph. 1, 23; Jn. 6, 56)
> In the end, when death is swallowed up in victory, we will
> achieve the prize, the goal of supernatural vocation in Christ
> which is the kingdom of God and his glory—God's heirs, co-
> heirs with Christ, our firstborn Brother. (1 Cor. 15, 54; Rom. 8,
> 17)

Meditation on some such summary or synthesis seems needed lest
we lose ourselves in a mass of details and permit particular aims to
obscure the grand design of God. The sacred writers themselves had
such a synthesis. St. John seems to move in the domain of God
revealing Himself in love. St. Paul seemed seized by the notion of a
new creation.

Particular mention, too, should be made here of the parables and
their usefulness in salvation history. Christ used them to make people
think, for their message was not always crystal clear though they
stirred the imagination and won attention. They still do. Here we will

find such works as Raymond Brown's Paulist Pamphlet on the parables or Harrington's paperback *A Key to the Parables* easily accessible and, I think, highly helpful in more accurately interpreting the meaning these stories should convey. Otherwise we are liable to fall into unnecessary allegorizing as did Origen and the great St. Augustine.

You may recall how the parable of the Good Samaritan developed in their hands. The man who fell among the thieves is Adam. Jerusalem is heaven and Jericho the world. The robbers are the devil and his angels. The priest represents the Law, and the Levite the prophets. Who is the Good Samaritan? Christ Himself. And then just to mix the metaphor a bit, the beast is also Christ's body which bears the fallen Adam. But I think you get the idea. We may admire the ingenuity and find no fault with the doctrine, but, as Harrington says, it is decidedly not the teaching of the parable, and I think it much better to determine that teaching, and then make its application to our times.

3. *The text should be interpreted in the light of the faith.*

(1) The particular vital context.

(2) The total context.

(3) The actual context.

Point one I am sure is familiar. It simply means ascertaining the meaning of a Biblical passage in its own proper context; for example, the historical significance of the call of Abraham.

Point two is concerned with the whole context, that is, how does, e.g., the call of Abraham relate to the entire mystery of salvation? We know that this call is the first of a series—calls of judges, of prophets. All these calls bespeak a relationship to God, and the point of all these relationships, the point of convergence is Jesus Christ. In him all are called to supernatural life. In seeking the whole context, we should avoid the superficial and look for the unity which God Himself has given to his whole revelation. In other words, we look for the permanent, trans-historical significance which is brought out in successive and complementary stages. Here we have the theme of vocation.

Now comes the third point—the actualizing of our interpretation. Abraham's call is the first of God's call to every man to faith and salvation in Jesus Christ. Further, if we see the kernel of the meaning of this call, then we will see as Van Caster points out: "An exterior lack of resemblance can disguise an interior resemblance which is profound; e.g. the modern missionary leaving by jet for the land to which God is sending him 'profoundly' resembles Abraham taking his slow departure by camel caravan." [16]

4. *The present value of the past event should be developed.*

This is briefly the problem of actualization, of making the Biblical event meaningful here and now to the congregation. One way—a principal one—is, of course, to indicate the relationship between Biblical events and our present day liturgy. For the grand design of actualization is to highlight the true relation which exists between a past event of salvation history and the present realities.

Psychologically and emotionally we can do this by our vivid presentation of the Biblical events—by making them live again. Some even resort to the device of staging the past event in a modern setting: if Jesus lived today . . . But this is not easy to pull off, and may easily result in a distortion. It seems better to spotlight the place of the event in God's plan and to stress the interior dispositions needed then and needed today.

Above all, we should remember our limits. We can present the words of God, and we can count on its dynamism. But man is still free, free to say yes or no to the gentle call of the Holy Spirit working within him. We can present the call to salvation. Only our hearer, by the grace of the Spirit, can determine his response.

FOOTNOTES

[1] Quoted in A. Richardson, *Bible in the Age of Science* (Philadelphia: Westminster, 1961) p. 170 f.

[2] P. Hitz, *To Preach the Gospel* (N.Y.: Sheed & Ward, 1963), cf. esp. 134 f.

[3] L. Grollenberg, *Atlas of the Bible* (N.Y.: Nelson, 1957) p. 27.

[4] A. George, *Listening to the Word of God* (Notre Dame: Fides, 1965) p. 21.

[5] H. Vorgrimler (ed.) *Dogmatic vs. Biblical Theology* (Baltimore: Helicon, 1964) p. 28.

[6] Cf. *The Historical Truth of the Gospels* (N.Y.: Paulist Press, 1964) p. 26 f.

[7] D. Lance, *Teaching Salvation History* (Glen Rock: Paulist Press, 1964) p. 30.

[8] G. Sloyan (ed.) *Modern Catechetics* (N.Y.: Macmillan, 1963) p. 3.

[9] M. Van Caster, *Structure of Catechetics* (N.Y.: Herder & Herder, 1965) cf. esp. p. 30 f.

[10] R. DeVaux, *Hebrew Patriarchs & History* in Theology Digest, Winter, 1964 issue, p. 240.

[11] J. Danielou, *Christ and Us* (N.Y.: Sheed & Ward, 1961) p. 66.

[12] *Ibid.,* p. 72.

[13] T. Maertens, *Biblical Themes* (2 vol.) (Bruges: Biblica, 1964).

[14] Hofinger & Stone (ed.) *Pastoral Catechetics* (N.Y.: Herder & Herder, 1964) p. 110.

[15] Van Caster, p. 188 f.

[16] *Ibid.,* p. 189.

The writer also acknowledges indebtedness to numerous other scholars whose influence will be easily recognized by those in the Scriptural field.

THE PEOPLE OF GOD

by

Reverend Geoffrey F. Wood, S.A.

Men today tend to use the term "people" in "a casual, vague way to indicate human beings in general." [1] For instance, when we say, "How many people are here today?" we mean how many individual human beings. Or when we say, "People are funny," or "Some people will never learn," we gather many faceless individuals under the term "people." Using the word in this manner we might say that the human race is an aggregate of the "people" of the world.

But what do we mean when we say the human race is an aggregate of the "peoples" of the world? We are not using "people" here in any vague, general way but with some specification. We mean nations. We mean that the human race is an aggregate of the German people, the French people, the American people, the Japanese people, and each of these peoples is something peculiar and particular, not at all faceless and amorphous. When the Bible uses the term *'laos'* or 'people,' it uses it in this sense. When we speak of the People of God, we have no intention of mouthing a generality; we mean a particular people with a definite history, tradition, with its heroes, its tangible characteristics.

What makes a group of human beings a people, a nation? How do they attain nationality? How, for instance, did the men, women, and children between the Rhine and the Oder, between the North Sea and the Danube, become the German people? How did their neighbors to either side become the French people and the Polish people? One could suppose that ethnic unity or similarity contributed to their formation and identification as peoples—Teutonic in the first case and Latin and Slavic in the others. It no doubt did contribute, but it could be strongly objected that ethnic unity or purity is no guarantee of

79

peoplehood. Where in fact is there an ethnically one or pure nation? The American people is ethnically mixed, yet it is still a people. Even the old, seemingly pure peoples—the Italians, French, English, Irish, Egyptians, Japanese—would fail the test of ethnic purity.

Certainly common language characterizes and may therefore constitute a people, a nation. It may help, but is it a necessary factor? Italian dialects, north and south, are notoriously different, yet we have an Italian people. Switzerland officially recognizes four distinct languages among its cantons, yet all cantons are populated by one Swiss people. From another angle, Americans, Englishmen and Australians speak the same language, but they are quite distinct peoples, nationalities. Common language and ethnic or racial characteristics may assist more or less in the formation and identification of a people, but they are apparently not prime factors in the process.

It seems that common locality and above all common experience finally constitute a particular people. Men within the same general area experience incursions, battles, the havoc of flood and earthquake, they pull together to meet some threat or share and exploit the soil, and soon bonds are strongly tied, community exists. Their common experience and the continuing and developing memory of that experience, embellished in song and story, re-lived in festival, give them sharper identity, a growing sense of self-awareness and pride. New experiences add their force to the old; song and story evolve into a literature and self-conscious history. Tradition accumulates, a culture flourishes, and soon Teutons become Germans and English, Latins become Spanish and Portuguese, Celts become Welshmen and Irish —we have peoples.

We may look at our own experience. Was there an American people before 1700? Some ask was there an American people before 1865! There certainly is an American people today, not established out of ethnic purity by any means, although one language has predominated. But the American people of today grew primarily out of a series of significant events within a wide but localized area. Experiences were somewhat colorless and meager at first, although later patriotic Americans did their best, post-factum, to salt colonial events with more significance than they merit—as George Templeton Armstrong notes: "being without the eras that belong to old nationalities . . . we venerate every trivial fact about our first settlers and colonial governors . . ."

But the Revolutionary War added a bright touch of red to things and supplied Bunker Hill and Saratoga, a Declaration of Independence and a Liberty Bell, George Washington and Nathan Hale and that ever cultivated betrayal of Benedict Arnold; it gave us Valley Forge and Yorktown—the events, the deeds, the men, the stuff of which a people is born. Certainly the Civil War, which has become an American Epic or Exodus over and above the misty knee-breeches and buckles era of Revolution, sealed our nationality—a bath of blood, an event of ardor before which men said, "The United States are . . .," but after which they began to say, "The United States is!" And then there was the great Western trek, an experience truly shared by the nation in fact or in dime novels, legends, songs, something "sacramentally" experienced in Saturday matinees and television drama to this day.

Event and memory made us eventually a people. Event and *memory*. The American experience requires that we underscore memory or tradition as much as event as a factor in nation making. After 1870 America received millions of immigrants who within a generation so well absorbed the American tradition, the memory of American experience, that they might easily identify with Andrew Jackson behind the cotton bales at New Orleans, even though their actual antecedents were hoeing fields in Hungary or fishing off Sicily or *attacking* New Orleans on January 8, 1815. Commemoration was as efficacious for them as actual experience for earlier Americans.

We have tried to show by way of introduction how a people is born and nurtured. It is understandable that a sense of nationhood, of peoplehood is a powerful force. It gives an individual and a mass of individuals a sense of identity, security. It gives them a frame of reference within which to see their past, present and confidently face the future. It contributes to their sanity. It is in our day a force seemingly more powerful than religion or ideology. It is questionable whether the philosophy of communism really excited the Russian people to resist and drive out the Nazis in 1940-45. It is more likely that a sense of Mother Russia really came to the fore and won the day.

Religious affiliation carries little weight when the *nation* is attacked. The French Catholic or British Catholic does not see a fellow German Catholic or Italian Catholic across the firing line. The Frenchman sees a German and the German, a Frenchman and they both leave their Catholicism for the moment with the chaplains, unless the chaplains, too, wish to pick up a rifle in a fit of patriotism and join the fight, as has sometimes happened. The fact that both are Moslems did not prevent Arabs from shooting up Turkish trains in 1917, nor did a common Lutheran heritage keep Prussians out of Denmark and Norway in the Second World War.

Religion—and we now stress Christian religion—which would lift men over their horizons, their limitations, and link them to the bigness of God and the universe and make them big themselves, has a difficult time competing with local attachment, a sense of nationality that is deeply grounded in memorable events, a rich literature and culture, wrapped warmly in the flesh of history.

But perhaps this weak influence of Christian religion upon the various peoples of the world is due to our unconscious and unnecessary disembodiment of religion, our unwitting disavowal of the incarnational aspect of true Judeo-Christian religion, our ignorance of concepts such as *Salvation History* and *People of God*. The religion we teach and preach to the peoples of the world puts itself at a disadvantage in that it tends to desert flesh and history, time and space. We declare our primary interest in *souls*. We wish to elevate *souls* to God. But men's souls by God's own creation are woven to bodies, to flesh and and blood, and men meander through time and space. Their eyes see visible things first; the invisible does not strike them immediately. Their fingers touch flesh, earth, monuments and not spirit immediately. Naturally, elevating souls out of their very element is going to be difficult and ultimately futile. We must somehow elevate the *whole* man, or better still, bring God into man's milieu. And after all, is that not exactly the tack God takes? He incarnates himself, transfiguring, elevating self into time and space; He reveals himself in events, in a place, in men, in a man—Jesus Christ. Somehow in our preaching and teaching we have contradicted God's methodology. We have undressed religion and presented men with invisibilities, realities he cannot see too well, timeless realities which cannot be dated. The strain is too much and men are more readily drawn off by realities, values that can be viewed, dated, that have their edge where the sun rises and the sun sets.

In one way, then, Catholic religion as we teach and preach it has deserted history. Religion is a matter of "me and God," the direct leap of the individual to God with concern for his soul's salvation. Hardly any recollection of Biblical events or people is necessary. How many have had more than a smattering of Biblical introduction? The New Testament is studied and sifted for items provocative of prayer, contemplative leaps. The Old Testament is perhaps as definitively closed as the Old Dispensation. A private morality, private prayer with a bland God and mind directed toward eternity, a gray realm beyond time—this is the disembodied religion we often offer, a religion that finds the historical, the sense-perceptible, time and space categories not too necessary.

For instance, what do we Catholics mean when we speak of *tradition*? For us tradition is not very much concerned with *events*. It seems to have little to do with *historical* tradition, the memory and savoring of salvific events in time and space. We adhere more to *doctrinal* tradition. We have taken salvation moments and persons and extracted lessons to be spelt out in dogma—theses. Our tradition is not viewed so much as a series of brilliant deeds of God, Exoduses and Falls and Jordan Crossings and victories over gods and tyrants, victories over all that is adverse to God and man as embodied in polytheism and greedy empires. No, our tradition has become more a series of decrees. Denziger is our tradition to many, the soul of the

Scripture, the distillation of revelation, cut free of distracting walls of water and Davidic dances before the Ark or the confusion of Jesus walking on the water. It is little wonder that men who are in time and space and find great attraction to event and story and symbol and learn much from them should find religion as we teach it hardly compelling.

Some theologians today would like to erase the notion of a God "out there," above us, and stress God as the Depth of all Being, someone who exists beneath all things and wells up within us to share with us his life. Perhaps there is an advantage to that, because by thinking of God "up there" or "out there," we tend to stretch in that direction, stretch toward the higher and away from the lower (and right away some false distinctions are made). God is high and therefore religion should be primarily expressed and appreciated by the higher faculties as distinct from the lower—memory, imagination and sense. Flesh, memory, imagination are too weighty baggage; they must yield to thought, speculation. Let the people taste joyfully and feed ravenously upon our concepts. God himself is divested of all that Biblical tangibles and visibles and experientials have put on, and becomes a geometric figure. Jesus is rendered rigid, undergoes scrutiny as to his natures and person; the Eucharist is fixed in a monstrance and the how of the Real Presence is philosophically probed and articulated; moral principals are set up at the top of the mind and even somewhere beyond, impervious to the contingencies of time-space existence, where readiness for challenge, an ever-ready responsibility are more happy, flexible moral equipment. It is no wonder that religion, made so transcendent a force, should have less efficacy than those forces which cloak themselves in the more perceptible, colorful, vital categories which appeal to the whole man.

Of course there is a popular form of Catholic religion which avowedly moves in a direction away from the static, ethereal religion we have described. But it does not do so completely. Religion will be incarnated, given flesh, blood, historicity regardless of the strain of intellect to take it and tryst with it somewhere above the stars. People will fix on religious *event*, religious *experience* and *personages* and cultivate the memory of them; they will develop an *historical* religious tradition to counterbalance a purely *doctrinal* religious tradition. No matter how much *salvation history* gives way to the *concept* of salvation in theological circles, men will devise on the popular level their salvation *history* after all. The unfortunate thing about this very normal tendency is that it stops short of true salvation history, true salvation events and personages—Exodus, Sinai, Moses, David, Jesus, Death and Resurrection, Pentecostal revolution, Peter and Paul and Stephen. It settles for more immediate experience and persons, indistinguishable from their own history as a people. They rebuild their structure from the present penthouse down to the thirtieth floor but stop there, leaving a vacuum between themselves and their Biblical foundations.

How far does the religious Irishman think back? To St. Patrick, his travels, imprisonment, conversion and miracles, to the missionary efforts of the Irish monks, to Sts. Brigid and Columba, the persecutions by the English, the religious and political resistance to William of Orange and the rest. A religious history does develop and is well remembered in song and story. But it misses its roots. It runs parallel to and is in danger of identification with a national or political history; it is in danger of becoming indistinguishable from the more concentrated and narrowing force of nationality. Spaniards have a religious history; but it seems to hinge upon events and persons dating from the wars to liberate that peninsula from Moslem occupation. Again religious history becomes indistinguishable from national history, is perhaps subsumed by national history; Catholicism becomes simply a national characteristic, a national religion rather than something truly universal and emancipating. And in this situation, religion only adds to division and enclosure; it sanctifies it! It puts God on the side of America; yet strangely enough allows the enemy to march out crying with equal confidence: *Gott mit uns!* It puts St. George in the English ranks to contend with the patron saints of France.

In any case, religion has weak motive power among the Christian peoples of the world today, either because it is too ethereal, fleshless or because it is so immersed in time and space categories, so blended into a memory, culture, and history which is national only, that it merely strengthens nationalism and cannot really lift a people above its own peoplehood, its own corridor of time and patch of space.

It is unfortunate that Christian religion must dissipate its power by an over stress on transcendence or by evaporating within the profane cultures of the various peoples of the world (a case in point being Roman culture?). There is no need for it to take either course. It need not soar above time and space. God's church was never meant to be a formless society, a philosophical or theological society, a meeting of minds on the topic of God on Asteroid 96 far above the teeming nations. God's church was set up and developed into a people. God's church is a people, the people of God, and we mean people in exactly the same sense that we used it of the British people or the German people. What constitutes a people? Events, significant, revolutionary, developmental events and the literate memory of those events. God's church is the issue of such experience. God's church is *Israel*—even by profane standards a people among peoples, with its exodus, victories, defeats, revivals, its trek, its heroes, its dynamism, its sense of destiny, its festivals and its literature.

When you become a Christian you do not simply enter a church body, a religious organization; you are initiated into a people. You make a datable, identifiable, memorable past your own. Your roots go now beyond the suddenly pale, suddenly less meaningful experiences and memories of your national ancestry to the experiences of Near Eastern nomads named Abraham, Isaac, Jacob, to enslavement in the Egypt of 1300 B.C. You find yourself identifying and glorying in that burst toward freedom we call Exodus. Yours is the grand rally at Sinai. You find yourself not behind cotton bales at New Orleans or charging up San Juan Hill, but marshalling with your compatriots across Jordan, crossing that Rubicon and occupying Jericho, Bethel, the hill country, struggling to hold on over many decades and then riding to victory with David and the prophets—Amos, Isaiah, Jeremiah. You find yourself wading through a rising tide of literature, sacred literature, that records and dramatizes the events you have made your own: the Yahwist tradition and the Elohist, the prophetical books and Deuteronomic history, the Wisdom works and Psalms, the profound thought of Job and Ruth, enough to match any Chaucer or Dante, possessed of an inspiration unique among the literatures of the world, ancient and modern; there is the Priestly tradition which makes the original swamp between Egypt and the desert a parted Sea —and why not?—it was a great day, a great escape!

You find yourself caught up with that ancient eagerness of the later prophets for fulfillment, the culmination of their history under God, a future king, conquest, growth beyond territorial borders, prosperity, justice, peace. You share the wilder visions of the apocalytic writers (wilder because so intensely desired), visions of monstrosities, caricatures of true humanity and culture, cast into the sea, while Israel, God's people, ascends—human—upon clouds to stand before the Ancient of Days. And with the arrival of Jesus of Nazareth you sense with all true Israelites fulfillment at last: a new Moses, a new Josue, a new David, a new Elia, the best issue of the whole history of your people comes to lead a new Exodus, to thrust you and your people into a new era beyond ethnic uniformity, beyond geographical patch or walled Jerusalem to universal expansion. He comes to thrust you and your compatriots across a new Red Sea into dimensions beyond the material, political, static, into God. He comes to give you a resurrection body, a body identifiable and circumscribed but radiant with peace and stability, capable of passing through doors once closed, through mist to clarity.

Adherence to true religion means insertion into a God-fashioned people with experiences and definability, milestones marking its way. It means insertion into and identification with a time and space framework that suits our humanity. Nor is this insertion merely mental. The sacraments take on new meaning, indeed their basic meaning, when seen within this context. Baptism is no mere washing. It is a living monument, a memorial of Exodus and since the death and resurrection of Jesus gives new dimension to Exodus, it is memorial of that passage, too. It is a memorial that really links the person baptized with the ancestral event. Each Christian goes through the Red Sea, marches out with those Israelite ancestors of the 13th century B.C., and communes with their subsequent history. He has a right to see himself at every stop along the way and he identifies with the passage of Christ on that later Passover, though unfortunately so many other fellow Israelites failed to follow to another shore that second time—and we await them still. The Christian eats the bread given at the Eucharistic table and participates in the manna feast of that ancient desert trek. He attends the Eucharist, too, as Paschal meal, reiterating that Passover meal that Moses held and thus the passage from Egypt to which it was prelude. But simultaneously and primarily he joins Jesus, new Moses, at his final Passover meal, prelude to his more evident passage from death to life—Do this in commemoration of me. The Judeo-Christian is definitely part of a people with a history, literature, traceable course, heroes, festivals, memorials which are sacraments.

You hear the terms *Salvation History* and *People of God* used much these days and you wonder—what do they mean? what value do they have? Salvation without a history is a mere concept—a wish, a dream. But when events begin to occur, authored by Yahweh who makes things happen, events in a definable area at datable moments, events that propel a people from slavery to liberty, from superstition to monotheism, from merry-go-round existence to straight line vision and thrust, then you have Salvation *History, historical* salvation, *actual* salvation, evidence of God who does *in fact* save. Salvation History is salvation incarnate, salvation in the flesh. That is what you preach when you preach Salvation History. And that means going into the details of it, proclaiming the many salvific events from the call of Abraham onward to the miracles of Jesus and his resurrection. You have an anthology of events, records of salvation descriptive of all salvation, even our own. This means knowing your Bible. But see whether it does not attract hearts, imaginations, and mark the memories of your Catholics more than general dogmatizing or moralizing; see whether it does not make your Catholics aware of their *true* historical past, that history which is touched by the finger of God and thus a more meaningful, enduring history and tradition than that of their particular nation and people; and see whether religious tradition does not for once give all other compelling influences better competition after all.

Of course, the particularly stirring and useful thing about your past as a citizen of God's people is the fact that the past is paradigm, exemplary of the present and the future. Looking back into the past you can see reflected your future. Your Biblical past is a mirror catching something of future reality, as a new Exodus. Other nations have only a past. Their future is uncertain. Sometimes a conservative trend develops: cling to the good old days; fix forever the status quo and write off newness, a future. This is understandable. But the Israelite does not fear the future because he has experienced something of his future in his past—Exodus. And he is confident, too, that a divine Person shapes his history, a Person unaffected and unafraid of time—Alpha and Omega.

We mentioned that there is no need to soar above time and space. God comes to us and shapes us up within time and space, establishing us in all the tangible, directional trappings of a people, communicating to us on our level, competing with all other time and space categories that would distract us. But we also mentioned there is no need to become evaporated in time and space, to become so *popular,* so incarnate a religion that religion is indistinguishable from time and space, subservient somehow to them.

God made us a definable people with definable past that can match for drama, reality, glory and vitality the definable past of any people on earth. And yet we are a definable people rooted in the dynamic love and fidelity of an eternal, undefinable God who simply IS. We are therefore a definite people with roots in undefinability and that means citizenship unlimited, horizons unlimited, vitality unlimited.

Paul Tillich defines paganism as the elevation of a special space to ultimate value and dignity.[2] Paganism is the deification of one spot, one place, one people. Hence paganism is polytheistic—there are many places, many peoples. A group of human beings desire to have a place of their own, a place which gives them reality, power, which feeds them body and soul—like the Swiss mountains. They begin to cherish this special patch of soil. But there are many such patches of soil; hence a multiplication of gods. Isolation, division follow. Men lock themselves in, unable, unwilling to pass beyond such ultimates.

God, the true Ultimate who is not limited to any one place, not encircled or identified with any patch of soil, reached into divided, isolated humanity and called out one group, Israel. He made a pact with them, nurtured them along as a people, gave them, indeed, land, a city, identity among peoples. But because he is the true, horizonless God, Israel could never really remain earthbound, border-bound like other peoples. Every time they tried to tie down their unique God, identify him with nature or the soil, he sent his prophets, men like Elia, out of the desert into the culture-land to remind Israel that its origin was over the border and there, too, lay its destiny. Israel's God was indeed "out there."

Jesus especially came to stretch Israel to new dimensions. He kept the framework, the meaningful trappings of peoplehood. The Word did not become simply Man—he became an Israelite. But Jesus invited Israel to step into universal expansion. Unfortunately many Israelites opted for space, nationality, ethnic limitation, the legal framework of the old tradition, the stone temple, a fixed city. Yahwism was national religion to them rather than the nation Yahwist. And those Israelites remain bound over the centuries by space, the ethnic, the static culture of the old era. But at the center the Twelve of Jesus, the little group of the upper room, opted for Jesus and Spirit. They stepped into a new era for Israel, beyond the ethnic circle, the Palestinian circle and Jerusalem wall, beyond temple enclosures. They commenced a new Exodus. They were true Israel and we are Israel en route again over a familiar route—yet a higher road toward new Jerusalem, new Josue running on before, new David waiting for us. Christian Israel is identifiable yet presses beyond space and time to the limits of the universe and, if there are any such limits, to the limits of God.

Ephesians 2:11-22 captures all of this pretty well. Paul is addressing Gentile Christians but he nicely keeps the framework of Israel present throughout. Still that framework is transparent with the frameless presence of God. Read it.

CONCLUSION

The points we have tried to make are these: in deserting the Scripture we have made our preaching either too theological, speculative, dogmatic or moralizing; this does not quite hook into the imagination, emotions, etc.; it has little real motivational force. But in forgetting the Scripture we have been forced to popularize or incarnate our message within categories that are too shallow, too *Catholic*—to use a term. We popularize by way of Infants of Prague, Madonnas of any number of places and nationalities, devotions of infinite variety, spiritualities that are French, Dutch, Spanish, Franciscan, Jesuit, etc. Our essential bigness breaks down into distracting particularities and pettiness—small, over-defined elements become ultimates and elevation is frustrated. We should preach Salvation—Salvation *HISTORY* which has an unction all its own. We should make our congregation see that it is heir to that tangible story, that it is part of the People of God as much as and even more than it is part of an Italian, French or American People. Once caught within that frame of reference, we must fix their gaze on transcendentals—under the Image of Jordan ahead and the new Jerusalem—Victory and Peace.

FOOTNOTES

[1] Paul S. Minear, *Images of the Church in the New Testament,* (Philadelphia: Westminster Press), p. 67 ff.

[2] Paul Tillich, *Theology of Culture,* p. 31 ff.

BIBLIOGRAPHY

Beaucamp, E., *The Bible and the Universe,* (Burns Oates, London).

de Dietrich, S., *Free Men: Meditations on the Bible Today,* (Westminster, Philadelphia).

――――. *God's Unfolding Purpose,* (Westminster, Philadelphia).

Fuller, R. H., *What is Liturgical Preaching,* Studies in Ministry and Worship, (SCM Press Ltd., 56 Bloomsbury St., London).

Giblet, J., *The God of Israel, the God of Christians—great themes,* (Desclee, N. Y.).

Guillet, J., *Themes of the Bible,* (Fides, Notre Dame, Ind.).

Minear, Paul S., *Images of the Church in the New Testament,* (Westminster, Philadelphia).

Napier, B. D., *From Faith to Faith,* (Harper and Row, N.Y.).

――――. *Song of the Vineyard,* (Harper and Row, N.Y.).

Stock, A., *Kingdom of Heaven,* (Herder and Herder, N.Y.).

Von Allmen, J. J., *Preaching and Congregation,* Ecumenical Studies in Worship 10, (John Knox Press, Richmond).

Westermann, C., *A Thousand Years and a Day—our time in the OT,* (Muhlenberg, Philadelphia).

Wolff, H. W., "The Understanding of History in the OT Prophets"— article in *Essays on OT Hermeneutics,* Ed. Claus Westermann (John Knox Press, Richmond).

Wright, G. E., & Fuller, R., *The Book of the Acts of God,* (Duckworth, London).

See also: First volume of *Concilium* for several articles on People of God and bibliography.

R. Schnackenburg, *New Testament Theology Today,* (Herder & Herder, N.Y.) for bibliographical material on NT themes. W. Eichrodt, *Theology of OT,* vol. 1 (Westminster, Philadelphia) for heavy but rich material—if you have staying power. Various new periodicals, e.g., *Bible Today, The Way* (British publication), Book reviews of the Catholic Biblical Quarterly.

THE INFLUENCE OF NATURALISM ON CONTEMPORARY SOCIAL GOALS

by

Reverend Robert Paul Mohan, S.S.

The word 'naturalism' demands certain clarifications. In general, naturalism is the theory that reality is understandable without reference to the supernatural. It may take anthropocentric form as in Swinburne's memorable utterance: "Glory to man in the highest for man is the meaning of things." As Vergilius Ferm has suggested it cuts across the historical stream of Western thought, although involving no necessary meaning and continuous sequence of historical development.[1] Irwin Edman described it as a tendency more than a philosophy. John Herman Randall, Harold Larrabee, and Roy Wood Sellars have echoed the same sentiment, suggesting that a similarity of outlook and methodology rather than a specific repertoire of beliefs characterizes naturalism in its modern forms.[2]

Robert Roth has maintained that no definitive history of naturalism in American thought exists, quoting Joseph Blau's observation that "perhaps naturalism is still too much alive to qualify for an obituary."

I am not going into the various philosophic attitudes of naturalism found in Santayana, Pratt, Woodbridge, Nagel, Schneider, Hook, Cohen, Dewey, or Romanell. Naturalism need not be, but often is, associated with sheer materialism because it has received its strongest impetus in a late nineteenth and twentieth century world when the empirical sciences developed with amazing rapidity, and reality was progressively identified with the concerns of the material order. Within such a framework of scientific method, naturalism's concerns are bound to be concerned with the world of tangible phenomena, but contemporary naturalism would certainly consider itself as interested in personalistic problems. Even historically, it might be added, the Ionians, who were perhaps the first philosophic naturalists, did not equate nature's forces with sheer materialism, as nature's components were thought to possess dynamic qualities.[3]

Father Roth justifiably protests the tendency of some Catholics to consider naturalism solely in terms of the deliberate corruption of the faith and direct causation of irreligion and immorality. He sees naturalism's development in this country as a twentieth century reaction to mechanistic determinism and idealism.

Mechanistic determinism in its reduction of the world to physico-chemical forces inevitably leaves little room for ethical, social or aesthetic values. The nobility of human achievement and human purpose would be lost in a determined world in which grandeur and misery would be different labels applied to a similar inevitability.

Idealism, on the other hand, in its exported post-Hegelian forms, posits a world which has either no connections or very tenuous connections with an empirically verifiable world of nature.

American naturalism is thus seen as a compromise, an attempt to preserve the creative values of the human order and harmonize them with the unyielding truths of a scientifically observed world. In such a view the naturalist would indeed, almost inadvertently, ignore the supernatural; but such a position would not be the result of a direct malicious assault on spiritual values, as much as the evolution of an attitude that philosophic compromise would demand of the naturalist.

Father Janssens recently provoked a great controversy in the contraception discussion by suggesting that while man's nature may not change, man's knowledge of that nature certainly does. This would mean, not the abolition of natural law, but a continuing effort to understand it in its deeper implications.

Similarly, the naturalist viewpoint would not necessarily be associated with nature conceived as invariable forces of matter and energy. Man can still have a continuity with nature even though he represents an unparalleled development in nature's system. What sometimes perplexes the theist most of all is the naturalist's regard for the social virtues and social justice accompanied as it is by a disbelief in the objectivity of value. But the naturalist sees love, friendship, loyalty, creativity, not in terms of divine grace and charity, but as purely contextual realities worthy of admiration for their own sake.

The frame of naturalistic reference is generally monistic and earthbound, although it may, in the idiom of Santayana, lend itself to a limited structure. If the natural is all, then the supernatural is an illusion, and preoccupation with such an illusion constitutes what

Nietzsche called a "nay-saying" to life, and what Marx considered a siphoning off of vital human energies which should be devoted exclusively to the world about us.

There is indeed a limitless thrust of human aspirations, but man must make his own heaven as he goes along. This may take the carrot-before-the-horse form of S. Alexander, in which divinity is merely the untraversed and inexperienced terrain that progressive humanity has not yet reached. Dewey and Peirce, for instance, would even recognize the functional value of institutional religion if it truly integrates human social values, but Dewey's "common" faith is eventually a social faith and involves not the slightest recognition of the supernatural and transcendent.

Raïssa Maritain in *We Have Been Friends Together* describes the positivistic climate at the University of Paris when she and Jacques were young students. It was a philosophy that was not as much taught as assumed. It was the belief that knowledge and reality were valued to the extent to which both were reducible to the tangible and dimensive. Naturalism is not preached from a pulpit or taught alone from a university desk. It is an atmosphere, a climate, a *Zeitgeist*. It is not even a mood that is consciously engineered but an evolution of a mentality that is the result of a cultural and technological evolution and the mystery of corporate human choice.

We can look at our world with enthusiasm, distress, or indifference, but this is our world and our time, and the effectiveness of our preaching will depend not only on our sanctity, our skills, not only on what we become, but on what our people are. And they are children of their time. Rosalind Murray once said that the Christian is far more pagan than he knows and the pagan is far more Christian than he suspects.

As I suggested, the efficacy of the preacher is dependent on much more than *his* intellectual and spiritual background and *his* mastery of the mechanics of oral presentation.

The preacher must obviously know his age and his people if communication is to be effective. He must see his hearer as people moulded by environmental pressures unconsciously absorbed as well as by principles formally taught.

Geoffrey Barraclough once maintained in a special historical supplement published by the *Times* of London that there is no such thing as a definitive history, for history as an art and a science must be continuously interpretive to generation after generation. We cannot pretend that we live in an age of faith. Our people are constantly making extrapolations from domestic political theory into the realm of religion. Exposition must be geared to the mentality of the people living in a free society who must be convinced by the most articulate of competing forces in their choice of everything from tooth paste to ideas. The pulpit is no longer the combined force of education, inspiration and weekly entertainment that it was in post-colonial America nor can it be a source of innocuous reassurance, fiscal eloquence, or extemporaneous moralizing in contemporary America.

The word of God in a world that naturalism has made is heard in a forum of contending ideologies. It must in presentation be technically equal to the skills of the advertising world. Plato's strictures on the worthlessness of the unexamined life strike a responsive chord in the hearts of the new critics.

Contemporary social goals in America concern themselves with the good life and a mode of happiness that will often be incompatible with the Christian message. Granted that the naturalist mentality leaves room for poetic imagination, religious and moral sentiment, it precludes the possibility of any fruitful inquiry that would take one beyond a structured material universe. Ernest Nagel comments that to the naturalist "there is no place for the operation of disembodied forces, no place for an immaterial spirit directing the course of events, no place for the survival of personality after the corruption of the body that exhibits it." [4]

James Pratt in his book, *Naturalism,* considers authority and institutional religion, reverence for a book or an inalterable deposit of faith fundamentally incompatible with the naturalistic spirit.[5] The acceptance of tradition also would be to the naturalist the fatal adoption of a "non-empirical" point of view.

I should like to emphasize that this is not a minority point of view. The naturalist has an initial advantage in concerning himself not with the more difficult problems of metaphysics, but with the existential concerns; and if we would tax him with providing inadequate answers we must concede that he is often asking the right questions. Perennial philosophy has suffered, not from intrinsic diminution of substance, but from a failure of its adherents to make it sufficiently relevant to the world in which it lives. Traditional theology is even more remote from an empirically-oriented mentality being less dependent on the natural resources of human reason. One need but remember Comte's famous law on the three stages in which the age of theology is pictured as the age of ignorance and innocence in which naive man explains nature by an appeal to super nature; an age of metaphysics in which he explains reality by the sovereign power of matured reason; and finally, an age of positive science in which he sees reality in terms of its ultimate physical components. Reason becomes as suspect in the age of positive science as theology became in the age of reason. Non-dimensive truth in the words of Littre ". . . est inaccessible a l'esprit humain."

In an age of ecumenism and dialog an aggiornamented Church will become increasingly concerned with the common values shared with the naturalist and the pagan. We shall have to avoid the sensitivity of T. S. Eliot who would see the greatest treason in being on the right side for the wrong reason. The elimination of war, disease, poverty, crime, and racism are contemporary goals which can be and are shared alike by naturalist and theist. And if our theology is what Père Malavez calls incarnational, we will be increasingly concerned with the problems of the temporal order. Our concern is belated but genuine. We have at long last learned that aloofness from the temporal order is laziness not piety. The starving Asian may be seen as a child of God possessed of an immortal soul, or simply a superior type of an evolved natural simian form, but he is still hungry. The Christian may indeed be a wayfarer who has no lasting city, but regard for the city of God does not necessarily involve contempt for the city of man. Perhaps in this world we have rented rather than bought, but we can still take good care of the property.

We can learn from naturalism, despite its essential poverty. Nature is still the product of nature's God, and only a distorted asceticism would see it as essentially corrupt and inimical to supernatural values. There is still mystery in our created world. Perhaps efforts like those of Gustav Thils' theology of terrestrial things will lead the contemporary Christian to understand better the flawed world of which he is a part. In many ways we have more hope but less immediate expectation than the naturalist. He sees human nature in terms of Rousseau's perfectible man not in terms of original sin, and the tragic disparity between aspiration and performance so graphically described by St. Paul is not capable of preventing him from lamenting over the fate of his world when his ambrosial illusions are shattered. How much of the cult of non-conformity, the theater of the absurd, the literature of the bitter young men is a reflection of the collapse of the theory of progress that flowered in seventeenth and eighteenth century rationalism? This was secularized optimism; it envisioned no beatific vision, but a human society that was constantly getting better. Turgot, Condorcet, the Abbé de Saint-Pierre proclaimed the new and better world as moving by an inner dynamic history onward and upward. Bury and Dawson have presented classic formulations of the pagan and Christian theories of progress.[6] But the idea of inevitable progress was one of the most enduring illusions; it lasted until the beginning of a World War that shattered the neat and well-ordered Newtonian world that Victorian optimism had constructed. It was the end of the age of innocence. Where there were no supernatural values or faith to fall back upon, the twentieth century naturalist often yielded to despair. The twentieth-century pessimist is the nineteenth-century optimist gone sour—because he had no supernatural faith to bridge the gap from cosmos to chaos. It is the pagan rather than the theist who is frequently more inimical to change, for his world is his all and he is neither wayfarer nor detached enough to contemplate a world *sub specie aeternitatis.*

It must be obvious at this point how difficult it is to distinguish naturalism as a specific philosophy from positivism, secularism, scientific or critical humanism. But it is equally apparent that the naturalistic mood is basically hostile to the supernatural in general and to a content of revelation and institutional religion in particular.

Nineteenth century nativism as well presented in such studies as those of Williams and Billington represented not an attack on supernatural value, but a militant sectarian theism which professed to see a threat to American institutions in an imported faith.[7] Know-Nothing-ism, the American Protective Association and the Ku Klux Klan were readily identifiable enemies and they were formidable ones. Father Thomas notes of The American Protective Association that "in the late 1920's approximately one fourth of the men of the United States eligible to join the Klan were included in its membership." [8]

These certainly were enemies, but Catholicism knew where it stood. Friend and foe were easily identifiable. However, naturalism today is a faceless enemy. It is no longer fashionable to attack any man's creed. Religion and the supernatural are not usually insulted; they are ignored. Overt opposition can make a potential victim vigilant. The quiet enemy is the more dangerous, for he presents the ultimate challenge in suggesting that religion is simply no longer important or relevant in today's world.

Christopher Dawson sees our crisis as essentially due to two factors: The acute secularization of Western Culture, and the revolt of the rest of the world against it. He sees our problem as one of sheer indifference, ". . . the practical paganism of people who have never thought deeply about this subject, or perhaps on any subject, and who cannot see that Christianity has any relevance to their lives." [9] The threat to a genuinely religious culture is not formal opposition, but a mass of opinion which is not anti-religious, but sub-religious. Modern man is seen as spending his life in highly organized artificial units—office, factory, union, civil service, political party, etc. The IBM card is his symbol. All of these units make great demands on his time and effect a great sense of de-personalization and de-humanization. After the Berkeley affair a cartoon presented a counselor talking to a student. The faculty counselor says: "I feel that I have gotten to know you better these last two years, A-125-250."

Marx once referred to a man (in his introduction to the 1867 German edition of *Das Kapital*) as an "economic category." Modern man may not be living in an age that is post-Christian, but he is indeed in many respects in our free society a manipulated man. Proudhon, the anarchist, once lamented that governed man is directed, legislated at, indoctrinated, preached at, controlled, assessed, noted, taxed, stamped, measured, valued, licensed, hampered, rebuked, reformed, arrested, exploited, hoaxed, squeezed, bullied, beaten, mocked, ridiculed, and dishonored.

The reaction against authority and obedience that we perceive today is not alone a reaction against a religious structure; it is a reaction against the institutional confinements of Western Culture. Dawson considers the sub-religious sub-human; he recognizes an increasing tendency to subordinate moral values and religious truth to social usage and to social convenience. He sees not only the absence of a religious dynamic in contemporary life, but an absence of any dynamic beyond self-interest. And he considers it vital to our society to recover the moral and spiritual foundations on which depend the life of contemporary man and contemporary society; to bring home to the people the truth that religion, far from being a pious and irrelevant fiction, is in fact "the pathway to reality and the law of life."

He sees the Christian as a man who must bridge the gap between secular culture and authentic faith. "A Christian culture is a culture which is oriented to supernatural ends and spiritual reality, just as a secularized culture is one which is oriented to material reality and to the satisfaction of man's material needs." [10]

When I suggest the religious dimension as one of hostility to naturalism, I should recognize that traditional scholastic notions of the supernatural are undergoing some modification. Perhaps the most frequently cited is that of Father Teilhard de Chardin.

You will recall that Chardin in *The Phenomenon of Man* broadens evolutionary hypotheses to include after pre-life, life, and thought a hyper life, *la survie* as he calls it, which represents a goal of meaningful qualitative progressions to a final convergence, a kind of coming together of all humanity. Matter prefigures life and life evolves to ultimate achievement in Omega. But it is to be noted that evolutionary process in the phenomenal aspect of creation does not rule out the transcendence of God. The supernatural is rather the end of man, but totally transcends man. The man who talks of becoming "more widely human and more nobly of the earth" makes a transcendent God the ultimate reality. "Let there be revealed to us the possibility of believing at the same time and wholly in God and the world, the one through the other." [11] The supernatural admittedly is not considered visually as a contiguous stratum, but in the more elusive imagery of compenetration.

Karl Rahner adverts to the inadequacy of the old image in discussing nature and grace. "The relationship between nature and grace is thought of as two layers laid carefully one on top of the other so that they interpenetrate as little as possible." [12] Again he says: "We must show that the supernaturalness of grace does not mean that man in his 'natural' being is a closed system and complete in itself with

grace as a pure superstructure which leaves what is beneath un-
changed." [13] He goes on to say that actual human nature is never
"pure human nature, but nature in a supernatural order." Historical
nature is not then an abstraction called pure nature over which the
supernatural hovers, as it were, but nature possessing grace.

Institutional religion is by no means hostile to naturalism as the
more liberal forms, such as the Unitarian and Universalist traditions
evidence. In churchmen like Rahner and Chardin the supernatural is
certainly not denied but restudied. John A. T. Robinson, Bishop of
Woolwich in England, in his highly popular little book *Honest to God*
suggests frankly that our concept of the supernatural "must go into
the melting." He quotes the martyred Dietrich Bonhoeffer's *Letters
and Papers from Prison* which contains the thesis that man is calling
for a form of Christianity that does not depend on religion, and
Rudolf Bultmann's theory of *Entmythlosogierung* which involves the
rejection of a traditionally concerned supernatural order.[14]

This new attempt to "salvage" Christianity amounts to capitulation.
Professor R. Gregor Smith says bluntly: "The old doctrine of transcendence is nothing more than an assertion of an outmoded view
of the world." Or it amounts to the anti-supernaturalism of a Julian
Huxley who says "My faith is in the possibilities of man."

We of course are concerned with the fundamental reality of the
transcendent. God may well be described as the "depth" of being,
as Tillich defines him, but not as divinity lost in the natural. Bishop
Robinson is preoccupied with the spatial aspects of the natural and
supernatural. But it is not a question of God "up there" or "out there."

It would be comforting to think that our people are unaffected by
the intellectual climate of our time. It might even be comforting were
the ghetto of which we hear so much to provide insulation against
the new paganism.

But a paternalistic spirit not only prevents man from living danger-
ously, it prevents him from living. The great words of life, the great
truths of faith must be made meaningful to a people who are exposed
to myriad hucksters in our contemporary world, and the ghetto is
not the answer.

Goethe has pictured the essential struggle of man as the struggle
between belief and unbelief. This indeed is our basic conflict with
the philosophy of naturalism. We either believe or we do not. God
lives or He does not. The pallid divinities of a naturalism ethic are
not God. On this terrain, naturalism is the enemy and our differences
are irreconcilable.

But in our social goals the story is different. The involved Christian
who has perhaps belatedly realized that theoretical commitment means
a life lived, knows that all men of good will can strive to make this
a more decent society.

For instance, in America where we have an affluent society which boasts a gross national product of over 600 billion dollars, there is another America, a sub-culture of poverty numbering in excess of 40,000,000 people — ill-housed, ill-fed, ill-doctored, ill-educated. "According to AFL-CIO estimates there are 5,500,000 'single person families' with income under $1,500.00." [15] The colored, the aged, the migrant workers, the industrial rejects, the alcoholic and narcotic poor constitute an entire culture of destitution which the pluralistic society must eradicate.

And consider the delinquency problem. In 1963 in New York City alone 40,000 children were arrested; since 1945 there has been in New York a 500 per cent increase in juvenile crime alone, and most crime and delinquency do not result in arrest.[16]

Racial justice is another area in which the humanist and theist for different reasons can work together. Nineteen million American Negroes have, as it has been said, demanded payment on a century-old promissory note called the Emancipation Proclamation. Justice in housing, hiring, education are not demands that should have to be made in a free society in this late hour. The Negro wants to eat in the same restaurants, stay at the same hotels, and worship at the same churches. Discrimination, as one of Harlem's 423,000 put it, "is like being punished for something you did not do." The absence of a socially-involved faith has indicated that the religious community lagged scandalously behind in the struggle for racial justice.

It is for the religious sociologists like Fathers Fichter, Thomas, and Greeley to spell out the sociological minutiae of these problems. I cite these few examples because it seems that our people are often more committed to the tenets of white suburbia than they are to the tenets of their faith. We cannot expect them to be other than children of their times, but they should be Christian children. James Collins has said: "The heart of modern atheism does not consist precisely in its rejection of absolute spirit, but in its counterabsolutist way of vindicating natural and human values." [17]

It is for us to know and compete against the countervalues of modern naturalism, a naturalism that is both within and without the religious community in this country. As a specific philosophy, it will be rarely encountered; as a mood it is everywhere. Its message will be spoken in varying accents, but it will always be the message of Nietzsche's *Zarathustra*—the death of God.

> I beseech you, my brothers, remain faithful to the earth, and do not believe those who speak to you of other worldly hopes. Poison-mixers are they whether they know it or not. . . . To sin against the earth is now the most dreadful thing, and to esteem the entrails of the unknowable higher than the meaning of the earth.

FOOTNOTES

[1] Vergilius Ferm, *A History of Philosophical Systems* (New York: Philosophical Library, 1950), p. 429.

[2] John Herman Randall and Harold Larrabee, *Naturalism and the Human Spirit* (New York: Columbia University Press, 1945), pp. 319, 355; *American Philosophy Today and Tomorrow*, ed. Horace M. Kallen and Sidney Hook (New York: Lee Furman, 1935), p. 145. Cf. also Jude P. Dougherty, *Recent American Naturalism: An Exposition and Critique* (Washington, D.C.: The Catholic University of America, 1950), pp. 1-28, and Robert J. Roth, S.J., "The Challenge of American Naturalism," *Thought*, XXXIX, 155 (Winter 1964), pp. 559-584.

[3] Cf. John Dewey, Sidney Hook, and Ernest Nagel. "Are Naturalists Materialists?" *Journal of Philosophy*, XLII (1945) pp. 515-530.

[4] Ernest Nagel, "Naturalism Reconstructed," *Proceedings and Addresses of the American Philosophical Association*, Antioch Press, 1955, XXVIII, pp. 8-9.

[5] James B. Pratt, *Naturalism* (New Haven: Yale University Press, 1939), pp. 11-12.

[6] Cf. J. B. Bury, *The Idea of Progress* (New York: Dover Edition, 1955); and Christopher Dawson, *Progress and Religion* (New York: Doubleday Image Series, 1960).

[7] Cf. Ray Allen Billington, *The Protestant Crusade 1800-1860* (New York: Rinehart, 1938); Michael Williams, *The Shadow of the Pope* (New York: McGraw-Hill, 1932); Oscar Handlin, *The Uprooted* (Boston: Little Brown, 1951).

[8] John L. Thomas, S.J., *The American Catholic Family* (Englewood Cliffs, New Jersey: Prentice-Hall, 1956), p. 102.

[9] Christopher Dawson, "The Future of Christian Culture," *Commonweal*, March 19, 1959, p. 595.

[10] *Ibid.*, p. 592.

[11] Pierre Teilhard de Chardin, *The Future of Man* (New York and Evanston: Harper and Row, 1964), p. 268.

[12] Karl Kahner, *Nature and Grace* (New York and London: Sheed and Ward, 1963), p. 7.

[13] *Ibid.*, p. 18. Cf. also on the problem: Henri de Lubac, "Remarques sur l'histoire du mot 'surnaturel'", *Nouvelle Revue Theologique*, LXI (1934) pp. 225-249, 350-370.

[14] John A. T. Robinson, *Honest to God* (Philadelphia: The Westminster Press, 1963) p. 23.

[15] Michael Harrington, *The Other America* (Baltimore: Penguin Books, 1962), p. 202. Cf. also Mollie Orshansky, "Counting the Poor: Another Look at the Poverty Profile," *Social Security Bulletin*, XXVIII, 1 (January, 1965) pp. 8-29.

[16] Julius Horowitz, "The Arithmetic of Delinquency," *New York Times Magazine*, January 31, 1965, p. 13.

[17] James Collins, *God in Modern Philosophy* (Chicago: Henry Regnery, 1959), pp. 388-389.

MODERN INFLUENCES ON FAMILY LIFE

by

Right Reverend Monsignor John C. Knott

It is my feeling and distinct impression that one of the character-istic notes of modern family living is an almost pervading feeling of insecurity. Married couples are getting so much advice from so many sources. They get it from the newspapers (Dear Abby). They get it from the monthly magazines, particularly the women's type like *Mc-Call's, Ladies Home Journal,* each with a pontificating expert. They get it from Dr. Spock. They get it from so many other professional sources, that too often the end result is one of deep insecurity.

For example, back a few years ago the big advice from the experts in regard to the rearing of children was that it should be done by a schedule. The baby must be fed at 2 o'clock. Whether he was hungry or not he got his meal at that time. His diapers were to be changed at 3 o'clock. Whether he needed it at 2:30 was beside the point. You did everything according to the schedule. This was a constant preach-ment that young mothers received. It disturbed the older ones, but the young ones followed it.

Now you never hear anything about the time-schedule approach in the rearing of children. The big advice today in regard to children is TLC—tender loving care. When do you feed the child? When he's hungry. How do you know he's hungry? He's got his mouth open and, therefore, you stuff something in it. This is why we have these toddlers who don't walk. They roll along.

Sometimes parents wonder when TLC stops and a little disci-pline takes over. They don't quite know. They are not quite sure of themselves. According to the number of magazine articles written on the subject the question before World War II was: how to be happy though married? Apparently they've given up on that because the question you hear now is: are you raising a juvenile delinquent? There may be something to it since some of our best delinquents are coming from our better families. And some of our best illegitimacies are coming from there too.

You meet with parents, you listen to them in discussion groups, and this is the one thing that seems to be characteristic of so many of them—an insecurity. They're getting so much advice that their concept of their own role as a husband or as a wife, as father or mother, gets clouded. They seem to be operating according to the last book or the last article that the wife read. The husband never reads things like this but she gives the digest version to him with a certain feminine twist to it.

Consequently, one of our great roles is to give to people—to our young married couples, to our parents—a sense of assurance, a sense of security. They should know, at least, the basic outline of their role as human beings, as unique personalities, as sexual beings, and as participants in the whole creative, redemptive and sanctifying love of the Trinity.

When you look out and see those people in the pews, you see them as present, physically at least (whether they're listening to you or not is another question); but we have to get home to them and touch them in the area in which they particularly need to be touched. First of all they must be accepted as human beings which means we have to be conscious of the meaning of the human being. This is true whether you're in the priesthood, in religious life, in marriage or in the single life. You will be happy or successful in any vocation to the extent that you know, accept and love yourself as a human being. You can't begin to love another human being until you have learned the meaning of a good, healthy, self-love.

We can go into the findings of modern psychiatry and psychology and learn a great deal as to what makes a human tick. But we with a Christian heritage can delve into some of the hidden meanings behind that simple definition that used to be in the catechism. A human being is a creature, composed of body and soul, and made to the image and likeness of God.

Every human being is a creature. This means simply that he's the product of the gift of love of other persons: first of God and then of the two human parents. Those three persons combine to give this human being the first gift of love he needed which was the gift of life. If it hadn't been for them, he would not have been born.

He comes into this world completely helpless, completely dependent on other persons, always on God and usually on His human agents. No matter how old he becomes, no matter how successful in life, no matter what honors he acquires in society, he's always going to remain one thing: a creature with a basic need to be loved and always dependent, to some extent at least, on other persons.

One reads these days about what is called the battered baby syndrome. Infants are being brought into hospital emergency rooms and doctors' offices with cracked skulls, concussion of the brains, broken arms and broken legs. One little boy was carried into a hospital last year with twenty-four different cigarette burns on his body. All these injuries are caused by parents who in a fit of anger or irritation take the child and in some cases literally throw him against the wall or bounce him off the floor. There is always a feeling of revulsion when you hear about those things—the physical beatings of children.

But we have no statistics that will indicate how common are the psychological beating of children and the spiritual crippling of children because the need to be loved has not been adequately met. So many people grow up distorted emotionally and spiritually because they have never had the feeling, never had the awareness that there is someone in this world who really loves them for themselves regardless of their faults and failings.

It is important to recognize that no human being in a very real sense has ever been loved in the way he should be loved, in the way he needs to be loved. Did you ever have the experience on a good morning of staring in the mirror and suddenly taking a closer look because you have seen something. You peer beneath the face you have grown accustomed to. You look in and there you catch a glimpse of that little old lovable you. Have you ever sort of stopped for a moment and nodded in admiration? You have seen something tremendous there and you grin back at yourself. It's a good feeling. You don't get it too often. In fact if you get it once in a while this is about par for the course. But there you stand looking at that little old lovable you. The thought crosses your mind: Why doesn't the rest of the world appreciate that little old lovable you? If they knew that little old lovable you like you know that little old lovable you they would be beating a path to your door just for the privilege of loving you. But they are not even using the sidewalk let alone beating a new path.

If you get that feeling once in a while it's an indication that someone has loved you in the past. We recognize our lovableness to the extent that we know that we have been loved. But there are so many people that never get that thrill of seeing the little old lovable self that is inside everybody. It is important to recognize that one of the things in preaching as in living that we have to recognize is this tremendous need to be loved on the part of other people.

In marriage this is one of the great roles of the husband: to love his wife. He has to love her particularly when she's least lovable.

On one of those mornings he comes into the kitchen and sees that vision of beauty standing over the stove. Her hair is wrapped in curlers, she has a drippy head cold and is clothed in an old housecoat. All this he has to take in even before he has had his first cup of coffee. This is the time she needs love most. This is the time it's hardest for him to give. He's willing to love her when she's externally the most lovable and the most desirable and not when she needs that love the most.

Oftentimes, it's the same way with her. He has a two-day grouch, and a one-day's growth of beard. He hasn't said a word to her in some time although he has grunted once in a while. And she has to love him? She has to if she recognizes her role. Her role is to be the Vicar of Christ, in a very real sense, not to the whole world but to this man.

This brings into consideration the other aspect of love. We are not only creatures with the basic need to be loved. Each one of us is also made to the image and likeness of God. The big question is: Who is God? There are whole libraries written on the subject but the nature of God can very well be summed up in a phrase of St. John that "God Is Love." We see that in storefront churches, the neon sign—God Is Love. You see it on car bumper stickers—God Is Love. We smile at that, but I think there's something in the very simplicity of that statement that's important for us to understand about ourselves and to understand about others.

Each one, each human being is not only a creature with a need to be loved, dependent on other persons; each human being is also made to the image and likeness of God with one tremendous urge: the need to love, the need to give, the need to be like God. This is part of the reason for the tension inside of human beings. We all have that creature need to be loved; we are all dependent; we're all afraid that there may not be enough love to go around. We feel a little jealous about the attention or time or energy being given by one person to someone other than ourselves.

But we also have that need to do, the need to love. I think this is the mark of the adult. The characteristic note of the child is one who has an overwhelming need to be loved. The characteristic note of the adult should at least be one who has put things in their proper proportion and sees that his main vocation is not to be loved. Stop asking the question: why isn't the little old lovable me being appreciated as he should be but, rather, begin to ask the more serious question: How am I loving? How am I doing?

This we have to recognize about every human being sitting in front of us . . . that we're all on the road to love. Some of us get sidetracked and detoured. To be able to understand the capacity for love that a human being has is to be able to encourage that human being after his fall to begin to step up again, to begin to try a little better today then he did yesterday.

This is difficult because every human being is born self-centered. If I were to ask you who is the most self-centered person you ever met in all your life, you might think of more than one person. But you might be wrong. The most self-centered person is the newest baby that was born in a neighboring hospital just a moment ago. For nine months he has been all wrapped up in himself, in a fetal position. You couldn't get any closer to yourself than that. The whole world for nine months, meaning his mother's womb, has existed just for him. He comes out into the world and he continues to lead an ego-centered existence. The whole family is centered around him, his needs and his cries.

It may happen at 2 o'clock in the morning that he starts yelling in his little crib and the battle goes on in the bedroom: "It's your turn tonight. I got up last night" until the neighbors call in and say: "Somebody take care of him." You might say, "Two months old; he doesn't know any better." It's about time that the parents began to lead him out of his ego-centric universe. Their role is to lead him away from his constant concentration on self and begin to make him mother-centered.

Too many parents with their own need to be needed, with their own gift of love to be answered, continue to love the child without recognizing that the child is not only a creature with a need to be loved but he is also made to the image and likeness of God. The role of the parent here is to be the image and likeness of God to the child and give their gifts of love according to this need of being loved but also let him give back, encourage him to sacrifice, encourage him to love, encourage him to do, encourage him to think of somebody else.

This is where so many parents fail in their role. They've been told that the child is all important, that the child's needs must be met. They have competition from the neighborhood and the neighboring parents who are constantly giving everything to the children except the opportunity to love. The parents break their hearts, their backs and their bank books to answer the needs of the child and forget this one reality: the child is also the image and likeness of God.

The child is born self-centered. Too often he grows up knowing only one thing: the need to be loved. At the ripe old age of twenty or twenty-five he falls in love and he marries the girl. He marries with the idea: isn't she the lucky girl! Of all the girls in the community he might have picked out for the inestimable privilege of of loving him he chose her and she should be so grateful. The fellow is serious. This is all he knows—what it means to be loved. He is taking this privilege away from his parents (after all, they've had it for twenty-five years) and he's doing it reluctantly because he thinks he's going to break their hearts. Actually they are the two most relieved people in the world. They've finally got him off their backs.

She, too, has been brought up the same way. All she knows is what it means to be loved. She falls in love with him and marries him with one idea: isn't he the lucky fellow. Of all the men in the United States (she's got a bigger imagination) she might have picked out, she chose him for the privilege of loving her. The two of them get married, fortunately to each other. They continue to love—he continues to love himself and she continues to love herself.

Take a look at a lot of the young marriages. They've got everything in the world in common—same background, same religion, same education, same this, same that—except for one thing: they don't know how to love. He has never been given enough opportunity to get out of himself, to love another human being. This is why so many young couples have unnecessary difficulties in making basic adjustments. They have to learn in the twenties what they should have been learning when they were two: how to love another human being. How to put this other person first. How to forget one's own need of being loved and be the image and likeness of God.

This is the role area which so many men and so many women, husbands and wives, do not know. They have read all the books. They have learned all about the adjustments of marriage . . . the toothpaste adjustment, the money adjustment, the sexual adjustment, the in-law adjustment, the housing adjustment. They are the best adjusted couple in the history of the world and perhaps the most miserable because they have never made the basic adjustment: away from one's own need to be loved towards the gift of love that answers the need of another person.

This is why marriage has to be for adults. This is why teen-age marriages have such disastrous rates of break-up. They are kids and they don't know what it means to love, to put another person first. Any marriage difficulty and any marriage counseling case . . . rests in this area: they don't know how to love or they are unwilling to pay the price of love.

We can encourage people in this growth of love. We can help this man understand that his primary role in this marriage is not to be loved. It is not to see his wife as the one who is taking care of the house for him, one who is cooking for him, one who is a good bed partner for him but to see her as another human being. We can promote the constant re-focusing of his attention on answering that one question: How do I love thee?

Her challenge is the same: to focus on him not as a breadwinner, not as a nice looking guy, not as this, not as that, but rather as one thing, a human being with a need of being loved. Her primary role is to answer this need in him and for both as parents to answer their children's need to be loved while at the same time affording them the opportunities of loving.

The family is the first school of love. It is the school which will have the most lasting effects on the personality, the emotional and the spiritual growth of its participants. Not enough emphasis is being given to the whole communication of love that is the essential role of the man, the wife, the children. This is true of marriage and family as a human institution. But we must understand and appreciate the tremendous reality that each human being and each marriage is something different. The engaged couple has that reality. They've fallen in love with each other for one reason, not because both are human but because each one is different.

Each human being is a unique and particular person. He is a unique reflection of the love of God. Each human being has a capacity to love that is different from any other. Not even our Blessed Mother in all her dignity and honor as the Mother of God, as the Immaculate One, can love the way this person can. She had her gift. She gave it tremendously for which we should be grateful. But each human person has his or her own unique capacity to love so that each one is a particular image and likeness of God that has never existed before. There is a sort of core personality here that makes him different.

This is one of the basic reasons why we have to reverence the individuality of every human being, no matter what his color or race or religion, no matter whether we like him or not. We reverence the fact that God created him uniquely. He has a unique gift of love and we encourage him in the growth in love, we encourage him to love, we encourage him to give his gift. So many people grow up so completely frozen inside. They've never been given the opportunity to love. There hasn't been anyone around particularly interested in the gift of love of this person.

For about eight or ten years I was chaplain in a children's home in Connecticut. About an eighth of the children came from families that had been broken up temporarily by illness. The mother or father was in an institution or hospital. The separation had little permanent effect on these children because the relatives were still in contact with them. They brought them home. They listened to them. They called them up. They came to visit them. There were the usual problems but nothing spectacular.

However, the other seven-eighths of the children came from homes that had been broken by divorce, by desertion, by alcoholism, by illegitimacy. One Christmas these children were going home. The nuns encouraged them to write out their cards and buy their little gifts for their parents. They floated out of the institution on Christmas

Eve loaded down with all the little gifts of themselves that they were going to give mother or father. It was a thrill to watch them leave with all their glowing expectations.

But then so many returned disillusioned, bitter, unresponsive, bed-wetting problems, disciplinary problems. The nuns gradually found out what had happened. They had gone home with all these gifts of themselves to give to mother and found that mother wasn't interested. She had a new love-life around the house. "Get away from me, boy. You bother me."

They went home to give a gift to Daddy, but Daddy had a new Christmas bottle he was watching go down with tender loving care. "You're interrupting a very serious work here, boy. Get away." And these kids wanted to give and there wasn't anybody willing to accept. They came back with one resolution: never again would they allow themselves to be as humiliated as they were that Christmas day. They wanted to give, but nobody thought enough of their gift to accept it.

One of the big gifts we have is to be willing to be loved. If you are walking outside and somebody asks: "Do you want a ride?" The usual thing is to get in the car and say, "Thanks." Next time don't say, "Thanks," say, "You're welcome." If you hadn't been in need of a ride, he wouldn't have been able to give his little gift of love. You're doing him a favor. You walk through a door, and somebody holds the door open. You are a gentleman, and you say, "Thanks." Next time say, "You're welcome." If you hadn't been coming through the door he couldn't have given his little gift of love. You have improved the image and likeness of God in him, if only a little.

We should be conscious of the tremendous fact about people: that they need to love, but before they can give there must be someone willing to accept. This is what happens to so many of our teen-agers. They have been given everything. They have been spoiled. And the parents have been driven to give them everything because this is the thing to do. They give them everything except the opportunity to love.

The growing girl with her bubbling womanliness and bubbling maternity needs to love. Her parents are not asking anything of her. So she goes outside the home and starts going steady often with one of the least attractive boys in the neighborhood. Does he need to be loved, and is she willing? This is not a sexual thing in the sense of physical relations. This is a sexual thing that she has a need to love. If that need were being answered in her own home the problem of going steady and the problem of illegitimacy would practically disappear.

One of the saddest things in so much family life today is a lack of communication of love. Husband and wife never talk about the important things. They don't communicate to their children. They don't listen. There's a silence that's worse than behind the Iron Curtain.

The more one is acquainted with modern marriage and family life the more one sees this as probably one of the prime evils. If parents do not communicate with each other, they do not communicate with their children. And how in heaven's name is the whole meaning of love gotten across to them? Some children have never seen their parents expressing love and affection for each other, whether by word or by gesture. Children have not been taught how to love or shown how either.

Each human being is born lonely, lives a lonely life and in a very real sense dies a lonely death. But each human being has his own unique fear, his unique loneliness. Every relationship consequently is a unique relationship between you and this other. This is seen most intimately in marriage. This is why marriage has to be a life-time relationship. The unique gift of love of this man is meant to answer the unique need of this woman and vice versa. It takes time to get to know this other, and generosity to give more willingly. This is what ties a couple in a happy marriage so closely together that when one of them dies it seems as though the survivor were walking along like a zombie. It is as if the whole heart and the whole life of that person had been taken away by the death of the beloved spouse.

For instance, take a look at a couple celebrating their fiftieth anniversary. After fifty years of more or less happy marriage they begin to look alike. He looks like she does and she looks like him. And yet bride and groom pictures show no facial resemblance at all. This is uniqueness.

The growth in love is not a *quid pro quo* relationship where she gives and he gives like a nice tennis match with a good volley going. In every marriage relationship as in every human relationship, there are times when one person will have to give incomparably more than either he or she is getting back and incomparably more than the other person is giving. This is part of the educational process of marriage. There are no two human beings who can ever go into marriage with the same capacity to love and be loved. One of them is always going to be superior to the other in a given area of life. One of them is going to be well along the road of love. The job of that person is to educate, to bring along the other person who may be particularly slow or a little obtuse or atrophied as far as his gift or need of being loved is concerned.

A couple going into marriage is expected to be going in with equal gifts and with equal credits and many times this does not happen. So if a wife can understand this about a husband, that her job is to lead him and to guide him; if a husband can recognize this about a wife, that his capacity in a particular area is greater, then they go in as partners with the strength of each other compensating for the weaknesses of each other.

Too many marriages are like the letter "A" with the relationships being those of mutual dependency. Here he is and here she is and they are dependent on one another. When one pulls away, the other falls flat on his or her face. Good marriages should be like the letter "H", two independent personalities joined in a union, feeding each other, loving each other, giving and receiving from each other. Each one has an independent personality so that if the other one does not completely or adequately answer his or her needs of being loved, each is able to take it.

Now there's a third element here which is very important. People in marriage are human beings and unique persons but each is also a sexuality. To understand this gift of sex it is well to be aware of some past distortions. One inheritance we have is a cultural gift. This is a certain New England Puritanism in regard to sex. It is accepted, but is hidden away in a closet. People don't talk about it and certainly not in front of the children. There's something not quite nice about it. It's not respectable and of course we are a nice, respectable family. We don't have that stuff in our house. The only ones that have it are the poor slobs and they don't know what to do with it, obviously. A conspiracy of silence surrounds the whole subject.

Those of you who are of French or Irish background—especially but not exclusively—have also inherited something from your spiritual ancestors. That is Jansenism, prevalent in the early seventeenth century. At that time the Irish were having more troubles. Half of the clergy were going to Spain for an education. The other half were going to France. Those who went to Spain came back alright, but they must have died an early death because nothing more was heard of them. The ones that went to France came back loaded down with Jansensism that says sex is dirty. Sex is evil, the attraction between a man and a woman is the work of the devil, and God only permits marriage because there might be a worse evil. They couldn't figure out what was worse than marriage, but they could not completely condemn it. Besides children had to be born some way. You get that oftentimes in the American Catholics in our generation. Their attitude toward sex, love and marriage is often the result of a shot-gun marriage between the Puritanism of their national culture and the Jansenism of their spiritual culture.

The pendulum has now swung to the other extreme. The emphasis today is on the physical aspects of sex. Miss Universe of 1966: name, place of origin, statistics. A girl learns about marriage, about sex and sexuality and womanhood too often from the newspaper and magazines. Her mother doesn't talk to her. Her mother sends her out to her first prom dressed in a strapless evening gown, the modern engineering miracle of the age. How does it stay up? No man can ever figure out. Her mother sends her out with this idea: dear, this is what you have to sell, so display your wares. If God hasn't been good to you, you can always go down to a department store and help nature along. And this is the girl. She sells her sex, hoping to be attractive. A boy grows up with only one question on his mind today: is it alright to make out? If he's a Catholic he might be asking the question. If he's not a Catholic he is probably too busy making out to be concerned.

Many teenagers have brought to a logical conclusion the error of a past generation. Sex today is primarily recreational. It is strictly a play project between two people. The only question is: are both willing? If each one is permissive and you don't hurt anybody then it's nobody else's business. So our teenagers today are recreating with sex without any real idea of what they are doing. In 1962 the illegitimacy rate among teen-age girls went up 104%. The biggest increase was for girls between twenty-five and thirty, where it went up almost 500%. At twenty-five and thirty they know the facts of life, but they have no idea of the meaning of sexuality.

The emphasis today is too often on the technical aspects. Pick up one of the modern marriage manuals. They're always talking about the adjustments in marriage. Chapter six is usually on sexual adjustments. The emphasis here is on positions, techniques, angles and manipulation. The logical conclusion at the end of the chapter is that the two happiest people in marriage would be two engineers. The love relationship between a man and a woman has become strictly an engineering project.

Now both of these attitudes, the Puritanical-Jansenistic and the modern emphasis on physical techniques, contrast with the real meaning of sexuality. He has a gift of sex, and she has a gift of sex, and this is something good. It was given to them by God and is not something dirty and demeaning. It is designed for one's own happiness, the happiness of others and the glory of God.

Now sex in the modern notion is only a limited physical thing with some emotional overtones because people do get excited. Against that approach we must emphasize what is called the mystery of sex, the mystery of sexuality. Man is a man not just because he has a certain type of physical reproductive system. This doesn't cause him to be a man; it only indicates the fact that he is a man. He's not only a man physically. He's a man psychologically. He's a man spiritually. He loves God through his sexuality, and he'll love God in and through his sexuality because this is an integral part of his personality. Every woman is a woman not because she has a different type of physical reproductive system, complementary as it may be to his. But every woman is a woman psychologically, a woman spiritually as well as a woman physically.

Every man by reason of his manliness is meant for paternity. Every man is meant to be a father by initiating creation, for example, with his wife in marriage, but always perfecting the order of creation. Through his gift of sexuality he participates in the whole Paternity of the First Person of the Blessed Trinity. Man does it in marriage by the physical act of conception. He does it also by his continual gifts of paternity and manliness to his wife by perfecting her and to his children that they might grow and develop and become mature human beings.

In the order of perfection, I think this last is the greatest challenge to paternity. This is where an adopted father is the real father. He did not give physical life in the moment of intercourse, but he continued to give of his paternity, his manliness, in perfecting the order of creation, helping this child to grow, to mature.

Every woman by reason of her womanliness is meant for maternity. She's meant to bear fruit. She does it in marriage with one child, ten children, fifteen children. She does it as a nun. A nun achieves maternity by perfecting creation in the minds and hearts and souls of children. This is her participation in the whole creative love of the Blessed Trinity of the First Person.

I have often wondered why women are not more critical of theologians description of the Blessed Trinity. They make the Trinity sound like an exclusively male club—Father, Son, and you figure the Holy Spirit as one of the boys too. "He" . . . . It was Pius XII who called the First Person the Mother-Father-God. All creative love is attributed to Him. For human consumption he splits off half of it, man, meant for paternity; and the other half, woman, meant for maternity. He says to these two sexual beings: "Become one as I am, perfecting each other and to your gift of love God adds his gift of love and you have the reincarnation of love that is the child."

We have to lift our sights up as far as sexuality and sex is concerned, away from the Puritanism and Jansenism of the past, away from the inadequate concept of sex of the moment, toward that one tremendous Christian reality. Through their gift of manliness and womanliness these people are participating in the whole creative order of love, not initiating it always, but certainly perfecting the order of society.

With regard to the subject of preaching the greatest attention married couples give to any speaker is when he begins to touch on the spiritual realities of their lives. Give meaning to the ordinary routine and their ordinary gifts of love and relate them to God. This is when they are the most silent. This is when they are the most receptive. This is when they are almost sitting on the edge of the chair, trying to get some answer to the hunger, the deep spiritual hunger of their souls.

Help them to see their marriage and their family life as a direct participation in the love of the Blessed Trinity. They share in the creative love of the First Person usually by initiating life, but always by perfecting it in each other and in their children.

They share in the redemptive love of the Second Person by all the sacrifices of self they are called on to accept that they might more generously answer the needs of others. As in His passion and death they may never see the fruits of their love, but as with Him it is sufficient to have loved.

Then there is always the Spirit of love to encourage their giving, to forgive their inadequacies and sins, to heal their wounds, to impart His wisdom and strength.

The great challenge of life is the challenge to love. The Christian does not love alone, but in the name of the Father, the Son, and the Holy Spirit.

CREATIVE WRITING FOR THE PREACHER

by

Leo Brady

Creative is a forbidding word. Sounds a little mystical in the non-mystical sense. Like necromancy. Or magic. Or culture. If we had it, we'd never talk about it. To be creative always suggests to me somebody going into a trance. Automatic writing. Inspiration: somebody breathing into you. How to be a yogi in ten easy lessons. Or sometimes the word "creative" suggests a tall thin spinster lady in a sweater with paints and pallette bending up from her easel with sweat on her brow.

All writing is creative. What we are thinking about here, I suppose —at least, it's what I'm thinking about—is imaginative writing. You make it up, but not *only* out of your own head. That's scientific or informational. You make it up out of your heart and muscles and emotions and desires and the pain in your stomach. You try to communicate to other people by means of images—vivid pictures—full of color and sound and tangibility—not by means of concepts. You try to communicate how you feel as well as how you think. Or how you feel while you think, since it is rare that these processes go on separately. A speaker from the pulpit is not making a factual report. Or a theological treatise. He is trying to form the Word for the congregation. To touch them one by one. He is trying ultimately to form them in the Word. A dry, logical approach won't do. The logic is of another kind. Creative writing for the preacher implies something a little different than a purely technical approach.

The technique is clear enough. Select a single topic: the talk must be unified. Start startlingly. Be clear about what you have to say.

End impressively. Organize. Prepare thoroughly. Speak in a loud clear voice. And quit while you're ahead.

The advantages of writing out a speech ahead of time are obvious. You can keep it unified. You can make a good start and a good end because you will know exactly what you are going to say and how you are going to say it. You have a better chance to come up with strong and precise phrasing if you work it out ahead of time. Wonderful, ringing phrases do not always spring to your tongue in the heat of preaching. More likely what occurs to you is something you have heard somebody else say a hundred times—or at least ten. And you are put to the trouble of trying to imitate—to repeat an effect somebody else once achieved, an even more difficult art than preaching.

It is well to memorize the opening and closing so you will never be stranded. If you do not memorize every word, at least you must memorize the sequence of ideas or images or movements—or however the speech proceeds. Silence is useful in the course of a speech as contrast . . . or as an implication. A pause may sometimes serve to convey what cannot be stated . . . what is too deep for words. But silence is an enemy when it occurs as a result of being stumped. Uh-uh-uh-uh has never been adequate, even for Tarzan, although his wants were simple. So much for the advantages of writing a speech.

At the risk of repeating some things you have probably heard often, I suggest this: make your time of preparation as long as possible; make your time of delivery as short as possible. It is my opinion that only a very good speaker can go for ten minutes. And only a great one for fifteen. Beyond fifteen minutes, you must be either golden-throated or brass-headed—or a teacher who is condemned to go on for an hour and does so automatically as long as he is between bells. A teacher has a captive audience enthralled to the mark at the end of the course.

Really, there is no such thing as a captive audience. You may be captive physically but you are free every other way, free in the spirit, where it counts. All listeners—and this applies in spades to congregations on Sunday mornings—have the gift of ears which is the exact opposite of the gift of tongues. Where the gift of tongues allows the speaker to leap language barriers, the gift of ears permits the listener to hear nothing, nothing at all. Sometimes they automatically turn off after a speaker says "Ladies and gentlemen" . . . or "Dearly Beloved." It is a form of lay levitation by means of which the bored hearer floats right up out of his seat and jets out of the room, to go wherever he wants. There are some sermons it is possible to describe as "sermons to meditate by," I suppose.

When you write down what you want to say, write it creatively. What does that mean? It means you must draw the sermon out of yourself somehow. Make it out of your thoughts and feelings and most of all out of your love and desire. Not out of your memory or your will. It requires a certain amount of inspiration. Something must be breathed into you so that you can say more than you would ordinarily say, and feel deeper than you would ordinarily feel.

Rather than try to think up a topic for a sermon, you must try to leave yourself open so that the topics which are all around you—in your own life, in the lives of others you know—will come to you, will force themselves upon you, will demand to be said. Poets and playwrights talk about this phenomenon constantly. The playwright says he thinks of a situation which might possibly become a play, but instead of rushing home and putting a piece of paper in the typewriter, he tries to get it out of his head. It's one of his tests. If it persists, he finally listens to it. He does not put a logical proposition up over his desk and then sit down and write, "Act One, Scene One," on his typewriter. Strictly speaking, one does not get an 'idea' for a play or a poem, in the same sense that one gets an idea for a scholarly paper. A creative work is not a concept to be developed and elaborated. It is something which strikes whole and entire and which then, by a series of cunning moves, must be trapped in a form which will enable it to be conveyed to others. Techniques are useful for solving certain problems. They have very little to do with the creative spark which ignites the blaze. Well, you see the whole thing begins to sound like fortune-telling or parlor tricks, tapping on the table and so on. The imagination works differently from the will. The will is a kind of mason chipping away at the stone to arrive at the shape. The imagination presents the shape whole and entire so the will knows what it has to do.

Be on the lookout for topics. Let them come to you. It's torture for you and for your audience if they have to listen to something that has been difficult for you to think up. The labor, the technical part, occurs when you wrestle the material into shape; it ought not to come in the birth. The creativity is free, bound to nothing, springing out of depths which it is pretty hard to dig around in with your bare hands. You have to wait until it presents itself.

But if you have to give a sermon next Sunday, how can you wait? Sorry, I have no sermon today: inspiration didn't strike. My creativity is not operating this week. End of sermon. Clearly you can't do that. So you work out a system of proceeding which will be there when creativity is ready to come; meanwhile, if there is no creativity, you have the frame, the envelope, and you try to dress these up in the hope that something will come and dwell therein. In any case, it might be helpful to consult lists of possible sermon topics. But I doubt it. I should think you'd be better off digging into yourself and trying to find what is waiting there. The personal element is the thing here, both in speaking and in finding something to speak about. A sermon cannot be like a salesman's talk, in which the technique is all. The achieving of the end is all. Something must happen from one soul to another in some way. Creativity must begin with something real: a worry, a revelation, a doubt, a help you know is necessary.

How do you write it? More technique. Margery Allingham, who writes mystery stories, says this: "I write everything four times. Once to get my meaning down. Twice to put in what I left out. Three times to take out what is not necessary. Four times to make it sound as though I had just thought of it." I think this is very good advice. Polish. The labor of the file.

But in what direction? What do you try to accomplish in these rewritings? To make the topic clear, precise, colorful, and if possible, unforgettable.

Illustration. From a very good book called *The Fundamentals of Good Writing*. Listen to this:

> Liberty is a very important thing for a man to have. It means he can pursue his own designs and develop his own fortunes and seek his own happiness so long as he does not interfere with the rights of other people. Therefore, liberty is a very important thing. I had rather have liberty than anything else because it is the basis of everything else. I had rather die than lose liberty.

Recognize the sentiments? But where's the style? Where's the right manner of saying it. Right? Well, most effective. The happiest union of sound with the sense. The accurate way of saying it. Patrick Henry said:

> I know not what course others may take, but as for me, give me liberty, or give me death!

It is *dramatic* in the sense of the abrupt and striking contrast. It is *rhythmic*: the right melody and the exactly correct number of notes. It is absolutely *economic*. Not one wasted exclamation point.

How do you develop a style? In the first place, it has got to be your own, but you might as well face the fact that many people have struggled with the problem many times and you might as well benefit from what they have learned. Read others. Your duties require that you do a certain amount of what we might call professional reading, in which rhythm and drama and economy are not prominent traits. But beyond these, read good modern novelists and poets. John Updike, especially his poem on the reality of *The Crucifixion*. It will help you build up a support for your own style and at the same time suggest many things to your imagination. Read J. D. Salinger and Bernard Malamud. Read Wilfrid Sheed, who is both a novelist and a drama critic—in *Commonweal*. Read Anthony Boucher—who writes Catholic detective stories, or John Dickson Carr, who writes all sorts of detective stories. Or John Creasey or J. J. Marric. Read Tennessee

Williams and Thornton Wilder. Read J. F. Powers and Flannery O'Connor, too.

In a way, I'm asking you to do this reading for the wrong reason. You ought to read because you enjoy it. All these writers may not be congenial to you. Perhaps none of them. You can't force taste. You can't pretend you like what you don't. But I am suggesting you read these books so you can absorb a sense of style: of the accurate way to write. If you don't like fiction, I'm not sure you can mend your taste at this point. But read them anyway, even if you don't like them. It might help your sermons. What you read may open up possibilities for you, may stir and prod your imagination. Did you see the cartoon which expressed President Johnson's attitude toward people who didn't accept his invitation to the arts festival? He was supposed to be saying "I don't know what art is, but I know what I don't like." But read Robert Lowell anyway. And Denise Levertov. And Kenneth Fearing.

Well, I don't want to reduce this to a booklist of my favorite authors. But obviously, Graham Greene and Evelyn Waugh. And Father Gerald Vann. And Xavier Rynne has a fine style, honed and tapered, I suspect, by the *New Yorker* editors. Becoming aware of style is a matter of absorption, I think. Not a matter of stopping and analyzing the structure of every sentence. Read and read. The rhythms of good writing will become a part of the structure of your own mind. It may be worth it, once in every book, to take a short passage and analyze it. Decide what the writer was trying to do and break down his work to see how he did it—if he did it. But mostly, I think you'll gain more benefit by letting the styles of others become a part of you. Perfection is contagious. It is, after all, a habit, and you try to hang out with the right people. If you are continually subjected to dull, inaccurate, flowery writing, you are forever doomed to that sort of sermon. Avoid it. Try to stretch your imagination. Try to grasp what others have done, and hope that some of it will rub off.

The question of observation. Literature alone won't help you form a style or write a creatively-inspired sermon. Sharpen your eyes. Get accustomed to looking sharply at everything. The business of the poet, said Ibsen, is to see. In order to report the truth and to write accurately about life, you have to look at it. As it is. As it appears to God, I suppose. This is what most great writers do in some way or another. Their work is not self-expression. It is an expression in another form of what already exists in nature. Look at things. Look at places. Look, above all, at people. Here I can recommend to you another book, Walter Kerr's *The Decline of Pleasure*. Most of us are in the habit of seeing what we expect to see. Or of seeing what we are told we are going to see. And then after we have taken the wrong

impression, we accept somebody else's categories or ways of classification.

Literature is one of the last resorts of the individual. All great
literature deals with individuals, not classes or groups. Today we
have got into the habit of drawing upon science for our knowledge of
people rather than upon people. We think (we have been told often
enough) that science—the numbering and measurement of everything
—is capable of more exact and acceptable truths than any other form
of knowing. We put people into classes; we judge a man by his profession, or his part of town, or his beliefs. The writer cannot afford
to do this. Neither can the sermon-writer. Even the good scientist
doesn't do it, I suspect. But I am thinking especially here of that
branch of psychology which is charmingly called the science of Human
Engineering, or something equally un-Christian. It is easy to look at
people and bury them in pigeonholes. It is easy to overlook them
entirely by bunching them together. The imaginative man must look
at every individual as an individual. He must never use words like
"personnel," for instance. It is the exact opposite of personal. The
uniqueness of every person. The humanity, the singularity, the uni-
city—all the words there are for this. We condemn the communists
and the dictators for being scornful of human life, for not separating
the masses into individuals. Well, the writer does separate them.
He does see the difference between one human being and another.
Or he better had. If he is going to look and see, to observe . . . he
will see the difference.

It would be wrong to give you the impression that such keen looking is tied up always with love. Artists are sometimes very objective,
detached, cold people. But they do look at their fellow humans and
at themselves. There is a story about a famous writer—which he
tells on himself—that at the funeral of a member of his family, he
suddenly caught himself, not grieving, but carefully and clinically observing his own grief in case he ever wanted to use it in a story. It
is not this kind of clinical study I am recommending. I am not proposing creative writing as a moral virtue. But as a basis for good
writing. Observation means first-hand experience. Don't take anybody else's word for anything or you will have to use somebody else's
words to express what they have seen. Look at rain, at bricks, at in-
candescent lights, as well as at paintings; look at people as well as
things. Focus in on them. Use your own equivalent of the television
Zoomar lense. Do your own looking.

The question of vocabulary. In finding words to express what you
see and what stimulates your creativity, you can also help in the war
on de-humanization and regimentation. As every person should remain an individual to you, and not become a cipher, or a number,
or a label—so words ought to be individual objects. You ought to

use your own words so far as you can . . . not somebody else's. Duck as much as you can the jargon of the day.

The battle against regimentation and de-humanization can be fought to some degree by keeping words valuable and alive. Words are in danger, not so much of being killed off, as of being embalmed before they are dead. Walking around being used when no possible significance can be got out of them.

The question of vocabulary. To write imaginatively, you have to develop an arsenal of words. (Warlike image.) A silo of words. (Farming image and a stretch for me.) I have no idea really what a silo looks like except from the outside. A stock room of words. No good. It's what most of us have. A quiverful of words. Arrows are out of date. Unless they are tipped with poison, I suppose. Tranquilizers. A battery of words? Still military. A font of words. A fountain of words. The important thing about your vocabulary of course is not that it be as wide as possible, although it's nice if you have a wide variety to choose from, but that it be yours. Not secondhand. Not warmed-over. Not duplicated. The Xerox machine might stand as a symbol of our day and even our cultural level. You can make copies of anything very rapidly, for so many cents a shot. In department stores these days, if you go to cash a check, a camera encased in a metal cabinet looking like a squared-off hour glass stands beside the cashier. A sign reads: "This transaction is being recorded for your protection." My protection indeed! Especially if I am a forger. It's for *their* protection. I haven't asked for it. A forger would be the last man in the world to ask that his picture be taken. But the copy must be made. We have passed through the age of filling out forms to the age of making copies. Carbon paper will soon be *passé*. Copies will be the thing everywhere. There will be no original and five carbons. Only the copies: duplicate it, we say. I can have the girl run off a copy of it for all of us. We are expert at copies. Well, this comes into the vocabulary picture—although perhaps you were beginning to doubt it. No sooner is a new phrase coined, then we must all use it to death. Perhaps the most encouraging thing about adolescents is that they still are alive to the wonder of language. Cool. Tough. Futures. Shades. Du. Patch out. Just a few recent expressions. Last week's that is. May be out of date now. But original. Imaginative. Now and then they lean over backwards and begin to manufacture words. Doesn't work out quite so well. Most of them based on jazz talk, or Negro slang, I suppose. But not copies. An effort on the part of young people to invent their own language.

I don't really recommend this to you. Too many neologisms obscure meaning. But at least we ought to try to get away from outmoded expressions. Dull, dead words that have no longer enough life to speak to us. Dark words without enough light to do any work for us. We are bound to be slaves of language to an extent. We can't really work out new locutions for everything. "Pass the beans" will never be equalled for succinctness and accuracy. "Hello." Can't improve on that. "Goodbye." Well, we could re-institute "God be with you." But there are a lot of phrases we ought to avoid. I am not thinking here specifically of theological or clerical terms. I will leave you to search those out.

The phrase "Holy Mother Church" is an image, once useful, that has been embalmed into a cliché. When it was fresh it was tremendously effective. Now everything is different. Even mothers. Freud has affected the phrase. "Dearly Beloved" is probably not even something you say to your parents or members of your family. You may love them dearly but you say it some other way. Do you even call your brothers "brethren" when you address them collectively? I doubt it. How much value does "the kingdom of heaven" have to a democrat—or a republican? "Choirs of angels" is a lovely phrase, but if we apply choir to the group of well-meaning but highly ungifted persons singing away over our heads at Mass, the force of the phrase is bound to be blurred. I suspect that even "Savior" and "Salvation" have got to be used carefully. There is a groove in our mind for them and they run right through like a train on a track and out the other side.

Test these outworn phrases this way: try to imagine if you would use them if you were addressing a single individual in the rectory. A lot of these hallowed phrases are now hollow, no longer holy at all. I suspect we use them frequently because we think they are safe. (Prudence is a word that now means cautious, close to the vest, don't stir anybody up.)

Well, obviously you can't make up new words for everything. But you ought to examine the ones you use. Check over what you have written and evaluate it. Try to decide if it says what you want to say. Clearly, if a certain group of words is a handy short cut, use it. The test is: will what you say make an impression on the listener. He's the man it exists for. Will it print itself into his mind? Will it make a picture there? Will he be able to see because of it? Or will it only bind his blindness tighter?

Another example from that book on good writing I referred to above. The authors are Brooks and Warren. What if John Randolph, they suppose, had attacked his enemy with these words:

Henry Clay seems a brilliant man but his apparent brilliance is really only superficial cleverness. He is vain and strutting. In addition, he is corrupt. Very corrupt.

Not a flattering picture, but not really very vivid. What Randolph really said was:

> So brilliant, yet so corrupt, which, like a mackerel by moonlight, shines and stinks.

He made his point.

Making a sermon is a creative act. You create out of God's words and out of your own flesh. It is not a mechanical operation in which you proceed with the help of five hot tips on how to get your message across—a fine old cliché. It is not like making a pulpit, which can be done by a good carpenter. Each sermon ought to be a fresh, vivid realization for both the speaker and the listener. Only imagination can make this possible.

PART II

REPORTS FROM THE RAPPORTEURS

PROCEDURE REPORT

by

Charlotte I. Lee

It is certainly necessary to begin this report by commenting on the fact that the 1965 Workshop was a very valuable experience. The mere bringing together of forty-three priests whose interest and problems were similar allowed for an interchange of ideas that was stimulating. Each came to understand the differences and similarities in other Orders, and much was gained in informal conversations as well as in the more formal lectures and practica. It was also a valuable experience for the lay participants, and one would like to think that their presence helped in the broadening of awareness which characterized each session. It was an excellent opportunity to share viewpoints.

The divisions into practica worked very well. The designation by age and years since ordination was a particularly happy one, since it soon became evident that each age group had different problems of delivery as well as more complex problems which were inhibiting communication. The blending of special interests such as missions, retreats, parish duties and teaching was a help rather than a hindrance.

The pattern followed in Practicum Number Three was flexible, but in general, the first hour was spent in an informal lecture bringing together some of the elements of the preceding day and the morning lecture as well as any matters of criticism which needed clarification. This was followed by hearing the assigned homilies, sermonettes or readings from the gospels and/or epistles. Three men spoke the first day of each assignment, three the second day and four the third day and each presentation was followed immediately by extensive criticism. After the coffee break each speaker repeated his assignment attempting to utilize some of the criticism of the previous hour. Obviously there had not been enough time to assimilate it all and each speaker was stopped frequently to go back and re-work a unit. The speakers were not stopped during the first run-through in order that the class and speaker might get a feeling of the whole performance and important aspects of organization and composition.

After the first day the class discussions went very well. There seemed to be a feeling of rapport which enabled the listeners to speak frankly about the impressions they received. There were no evidences of vindictiveness, and the criticism seemed to be accepted readily.

After completing the first round of assignments the group began a rotation of rapporteurs. Those attending Practica Number Three prepared oral interpretations of the liturgical or Biblical selections. This assignment, while it did not perhaps strictly follow the original plan for the Workshop, seemed to be a popular and desired addition. There was considerable interest in the position and purpose of the gospels and epistles in the new concept of the Mass.

Since there was only a single day for each group, three men would speak, and then there would be a period of criticism, followed by three more with criticism; finally the remainder of the group would present their assignments, and the class would criticize. The grouping facilitated criticism because there were many problems in common. Moreover, it permitted the completion of all the assignments without spending undue time on any individual one at the expense of others. Psychologically it helped alleviate tension on the part of the later speakers.

The use of the tape recorders was an excellent idea. Most participants recorded not only their assignments but the criticism and discussion as well. The video tape sessions were traumatic but invaluable. The impact of seeing and hearing themselves was lasting and made subsequent criticism much more pointed. It was found that carefully guided discussion was needed after each session, however, particularly with the two more mature groups whose self-confidence seemed somewhat shattered. Some time was spent in reviewing class criticism and making it specifically applicable to the faults seen and heard on video tape.

The problems which emerged most clearly with the group who were thirty-five to forty-three years old seemed to center in four areas. First, they were having difficulty making the transfer from what they had always considered a perfectly acceptable "Sunday Sermon" to the requirements of a "Homily." They began to feel certain restrictions when they spoke of "homilies." This was undoubtedly a healthy thing and may well result in a re-examination of their function in communicating to their congregations.

The first bears directly upon the second area of difficulty. It became evident that more time and care was needed in organization and

composition. Clearly, some of the first assignments had not been prepared in advance and suffered from lack of focal points, climaxes and
adequate application to the situation for which they were intended.
Several members used general outlines, or even vague ideas, which had
worked before. After the first two days this problem improved, but
there was still the pressure of time and the dangerous idea that because one knows what one wishes to talk about and has talked on the
subject often before, there is no need to make formal preparation.
There was a strong impression that some of the homilies were not
only taken from a deep freeze where they had been reposing since
the year before, but that they had been originally stored there immediately after ordination. In the discussion emphasis was placed on
the changing format of the service and especially on the need to meet
contemporary situations as they confront the laymen of the congregation.

The third major problem was a very real need for vocal and physical
technique. Most of the priests had had little or no voice work and
had not used what they had once learned. Voice placement was a
common difficulty. Many were straining their voices by pushing from
the tops of their throats or letting a deep voice rumble in their chests.
Almost without exception they needed work on breathing both for
support of tone and for control of volume. Inflection ranges were
limited, which is, of course, partially a result of faulty placement and
inadequate breath control. Gestures tended to be either random or
autistic or totally lacking. It seemed clearly indicated that most of the
group had given no attention to their "instruments of communication."

The fourth area of difficulty was perhaps the most complex and
most basic and the problem of which the other three are symptomatic.
The thirty-five to forty-three years old group and the next more mature group seemed to be particularly plagued by the "changing image"
which they are asked to develop, especially in the pulpit and at the
altar. Some seem to have been trained that the priest should not
establish any direct eye contact with the people during the Mass
itself, and thus the participation of the laity in prayers and responses
was causing some self-consciousness and discomfort. Even more critical was the question of the priests' responsibilities and function during
the homily.

The above difficulty came into sharpest focus in regard to the reading of the gospels. Almost without exception the three more mature
groups were troubled by a confusion in their own minds between a
performance and active communication of the material in question.
The youngest group seemed to feel quite at ease with their role. It
was necessary to spend considerable time in attempting to clarify the
differences between a "dramatic presentation" and a vivid, meaningful reading of "Biblical literature." The approach which emphasized
the importance of the word of God and the disadvantage of familiarity

for the congregation seemed to help some. Attention was given to whatever elements of narration were present and the reverent, and yet vital, handling of direct discourse. The problem of decorum needs further clarification as does the need for structural and "literary" analysis before attempting to read aloud.

PROCEDURE REPORT

by

T. J. Spencer

As any textbook on the subject will reveal, techniques of oral communication are difficult to discuss in writing. Yet a good part of the discussion in Practicum Number Four (and in the other practica that I met) centered on just these techniques. We encountered some predictable problems: poor placement, nasality, loss of voice at the ends of phrases, tight jaw, monotonous pitch, and so on. In each case, the problems and the principles underlying their solution were discussed with the whole group alongside the practical work with the individual preacher.

What can be more clearly reported in writing is the discussion of those faults in both preparation and execution common to speech and writing. The following topics arose from the practical needs of the participants.

CLERICAL TONE

It was necessary for us first to define tone as "that quality which lets the listener know how to take what is said." We emphasized that any utterance, and therefore any homily, has *some* kind of tone, ideally, under the control of the speaker. A speaker usually knows when his tone is ironic, for example, but if he sounds patronizing, it is probably not because he wants to.

Clerical tone we defined as "that quality, arising from many sources, which lets the listener know that the speaker is less interested in relating what is said to the listener, than in his own relation to the speaking situation itself." The commonest and most offensive example of it is in the preacher who seems to pontificate, to have a reverence

131

for his own person that at the same time implies a contempt for his congregation.

The most obvious source of clerical tone, then, is the actuality of what the tone seems to imply; when the preacher really *is* more concerned with himself as preacher than with preaching the word of God to his congregation, the congregation knows it.

Among the other sources of clerical tone are many things objectionable in themselves and others which are innocuous enough except in so far as their constant repetition makes them mannerisms. Among the latter are three varieties of obtrusive phraseology, expressions which call attention to themselves by their oddity.

The first of these three kinds is the "printed page expression." By this term I mean to include all phrases which are proper enough in writing but hardly ever heard in any spoken dialect of the language: "so too we," "surely we all have," and so on. (I recognize that the meanings of these expressions may be as responsible for the peculiar tone as their artificality of speech.)

A second group of obtrusive phrases is the sentimental. Such expressions as "deep down inside" are only occasionally justifiable and always distracting. Many preachers have their own collections of such easy and vague implications of an interior life, and they often use them to excess.

The third group of offensive expressions is the stressed citation of authority. There is nothing wrong in quoting Saint Thomas either in a homily or in a scholarly paper; what *is* wrong is putting more vocal stress on "as Saint Thomas tells us" than on what Saint Thomas said.

Most of the topics which follow have also their bearing on clerical tone.

THE TYPICAL STORY

Storytelling in general is a weak homiletic technique. If the homily is an explication of a gospel story, then telling another story doesn't explain much, and "introductory" stories distract from the gospel word. Even if the story is a "true experience" of the preacher, the congregation accepts it as a work of fiction and unconsciously judges it as one. Most preachers do not fare well as authors of fiction.

The most objectionable story, however, is the one with such unspecified leading characters as The Husband, The Layman, One, You, The Good Christian, and so on. Preachers sometimes adopt these stories because they are reminiscent of Christ's own parables. That is exactly what is wrong with them; they have the form of Christ's parables (or a shadow of it) but neither the content nor the impact.

At the root of this difficulty is the preacher's frequent tendency actually to think of the world as operating typically in accordance with these nascent myths. It is their simple-minded behavioral analysis as much as their form which offends. As with clerical tone, the positive corrective for this difficulty (as opposed to the negative: avoiding them) is to focus sharply on the real needs, the real character, the real world of the congregation.

EXAMPLES

The typical stories we have just discussed often function as so-called examples (although they often exemplify nothing so much as the preacher's poverty of imagination). The same can be said of other "examples"; not examples in the scientific sense of specific illustrations, but those frequent allusions to the quasi-particular, introduced more for their supposed interest-arousing effect than for any pertinence to the theme of the homily. Far from arousing interest, they are often so remote from the main subject or liturgical ground of the homily as to be totally distracting.

Another danger arises from the fact that even properly used examples can be weakened by multiplication. The listener gets just as tired of hearing the same principle exemplified three times as he does of hearing anything stated three different ways. This latter practice (of rephrasing every idea and repeating it two or three times) is sometimes cultivated by preachers in the mistaken belief that they are thereby achieving clarity. Constant restatement leads, not to clarity, but to confusion.

EXTENDED METAPHOR

Ultimate confusion is also likely to be the product of such extended metaphors as some preachers are wont to use. By these I mean to include most rhetorical analogies. Metaphor is itself a doubtful homiletic device, like storytelling and for similar reasons; extended metaphor shares in that weakness and has disadvantages of its own.

The greatest difficulty in the use of such metaphors lies, not in the sense of corniness that modern congregations feel when hearing them, but in the tendency of their meaning to get away from the speaker's control. One of our workshop preachers, for example, began by condemning the stupidity of the moth who circles the flame, went from there to the worthlessness of the flame (symbolizing the glitter of worldly goals), and concluded by pleading for a God-centered life, unintentionally but inescapably suggesting that such a life would be just as stupid, so far as our (moth-like) behavior is concerned.

UNITY AND SIMPLICITY

Impelled by a desire to touch on all points of Christian dogma in the course of a liturgical year, or to draw out of a Scriptural passage all meaningful inferences, or simply to fill twenty minutes, many preachers give a succession of sermons, loosely connected, rather than a homily. Trying to make more than one point results in making none of them well. Preachers often seem to go from Scriptural exegesis to personal experience to modern application to examination of conscience to exhortation, unaware that most of what they are doing is anti-climactic. (This general organizational difficulty parallels what Mr. Brady has called the "symphonic ending" of the sermon.) Sometimes the fault here lies in excessive organization before the fact; in outlining all the points that might be made and then preparing a homily which makes them, utterly disregarding the effects of any of them.

CONNECTIONS AND TRANSITIONS

Apparently preachers have the habit of putting more energy into finding and developing points to be made than in relating points one to another. It was necessary for us to emphasize that the preacher must lead the congregation in thought, not think for it. All too often, a preacher will in effect say that A suggests to him B which in turn leads to C, while the congregation sees no connection whatsoever between A, B, and C or any reason for the preacher's mentioning any of them. A constant theme of our sessions was the necessity of recognizing and using the thoughts of the congregation as a principle of order, not the subjective associative logic of the preacher.

CONCLUSIONS

I think it is a fair conclusion from our experience in Practicum Number Four that seminary training in homiletics is often superficial at best, and wrong-headed at worst. It positively encourages a concentration on the preacher's own person and mission that implies a contempt for the congregation reminiscent of the medieval distinction between clergy and laity. Its rhetorical techniques are a mixture of outmoded classicism and crass, modern salesmanship. Its goals are remote from both the congregation and the liturgy.

At this vital point in the history of the Church, nothing is so badly needed as realistic and imaginative homiletic practice; training of the same order is the only cause that will produce that effect.

SPEECH, VOICE, AND HEARING PROBLEMS OF PRIEST-PARTICIPANTS

by

Eugene L. Walle

In this report, the writer will describe: (1) the format of referral and speech and hearing examinations including the testing equipment and environmental conditions of examinations, (2) the procedures developed for reports and the immediate follow-up of examinations and therapies, (3) the classification of the communication problems detected according to a national system or nomenclature of communicative disorders, (4) the patterning of general recommendations and procedures established for long-range carry-over stemming from evaluations and therapies.

FORMAT OF REFERRAL AND EXAMINATIONS

Directives to the four skilled rapporteurs of the four practica sections from the workshop director were to advise each priest to seek special speech and hearing examinations and therapies if such were warranted. Thus, a judgment factor in terms of a deviation from what was considered normal speech was requested from a select and highly qualified staff in the field of communication arts. Arrangements were also advised for those priests to seek the services of the consultant in speech and hearing on a purely voluntary basis. Prior to the workshop, special speech, voice, and hearing forms and examination procedures were prepared so that information obtained could be systematized and distributed during the time of the practica sessions. Time periods for examinations were initally estimated to range from thirty to sixty minutes but dependent entirely upon whatever

135

problem was detected. The battery of tests developed and used throughout the workshop were conducted at The Catholic University Speech and Hearing Clinic. Tests included pure tone and bone clinical audiometry, speech audiometry conducted in dual sound room conditions using a standard battery of procedures (Most Comfortable Listening Level for right, left, and both ears; a Speech Reception Threshold or ability to perceive faint speech; Discrimination Testing or the measurement of the abilty to hear and interpret critically balanced lists of words and phrases; Signal-Noise Ratio testing or measurements of the ability to perceive and interpret speech in difficult listening situations; and Discomfort Level or tolerance of sound presented at high level of intensity). Speech and voice testing included a phonetically balanced reading paragraph with readings recorded on a high fidelity tape recorder, standard clinical articulation tests and examinations of oral motor coordination skills of the lips, tongue, and velum, pitch range of voice, intensity of voice measurements, rate and inflectional patterning of voice, tests for breathing during speech, and voice quality estimates. Results were recorded on forms prepared in advance of the workshop. Each priest was also requested to fill out a short questionnaire for case history purposes particularly emphasizing previous medical or paramedical care or attention to the speech and/or hearing functions.

PROCEDURAL STRUCTURE FOLLOWING EXAMINATION

After each examination of the speech, hearing, and voice functions, a report was prepared on each priest covering salient features of results of testing as well as recommendations (immediate and long-range advice). Multiple copies of reports were made and provided the rapporteur of a given practicum section, the workshop director, and the priest examined. These results were provided within a twenty-four hour period following examination in the attempt to provide information as quickly as possible in the hope that some benefit could be derived during the remaining practica sessions. Of the total of forty-three (43) priests enrolled in the workshop, seventeen (17) received speech, hearing, and voice examinations. Of the seventeen, fourteen (14) were evaluated on a direct referral from rapporteurs and three (3) were seen on a self-referral basis. The age range of the seventeen priests was from 27 to 57 years of age with a mean of 38.8 years. The cluster of age range was significant between 27-38 years giving a number of 11 men in this age bracket; 6 men were evaluated between the age range of 43 to 57 years. A listing of the number of priests and their age is given below:

Number of Priests	*Age in Whole Years*
1	27 years of age
3	28 years of age

1	30 years of age
1	32 years of age
2	33 years of age
1	34 years of age
1	36 years of age
1	38 years of age
1	43 years of age
1	44 years of age
2	51 years of age
2	57 years of age

Total: 17   Mean in Years: 38.8

A total of forty (40) appointments were made which included both examination periods and times for scheduling direct clinical therapy. A break-down of the 40 appointments during the Workshop period gives a better idea of number of men seen together with the clustering of attention to the individual's problem.

Number of Priests	Instances Seen Throughout Workshop
1	5
3	4
9	2
5	1

NOMENCLATURE USED

The *Rehabilitation Codes* nomenclature of Communicative Disorders was used as a basis for classifying the problems.[1] In general, the communicative problems assessed were mild but with several instances of clinically significant disorders requiring more than short term consultation and therapy. The clinical nomenclature used by the writer is divided into three areas of impairment: hearing function, speech function, and voice function.

Impairment of Hearing Function

Normal hearing is defined as consisting of sensitivity to and the transmission and recognition of sounds within appropriate environmental limits.[2] Ranges of sensitivity are based on a scale of decibels of hearing for speech related to normal acuity. The following coding with clinical implications were made for the following men:

(1) Four (4) individuals had a *reduction of sensitivity of hearing* for speech in the 228 binaural or two ear classification code which ranges in loss from 27-44 decibels. The significant finding here is a near or complete loss for soft speech (whisper, soft spoken speech and conversation). With one priest with added problems, of a monotone voice and inadequate intensity control

or monitoring, the difficulty was directly related to the two ear hearing difficulty.

(2) Three (3) priests had a binaural or *two ear hearing acuity reduction* coded in the 227 classification range between 16-26 decibels. Such problems are not too clinically significant but as with (1) above, such problems warranted medical follow-up, periodic reevaluations and attention to visual cues to assist in maximum reception of speech as well as maximum seating arrangements during critical listening.

(3) One (1) priest had a mild but clinically significant right ear *conductive hearing loss* of long origin coded as 247.

(4) One (1) priest had coded 249 *right ear nerve type problem* in the range of 67-84 decibels indicating a severe hearing impairment to that ear. Added problems included an inability to localize sound due to essentially one ear hearing, slightly reduced acuity in the "better" or left ear, and difficulty in the ability to perceive speech in noise background situations. Speech deterioration was beginning to manifest itself with distortions of sibilant sounds (s, z, zh, sh).

(5) Two (2) priests were coded as having a binaural or two ear 242 classification indicating a slight hearing reduction in the ability to adequately preceive and interpret critical sounds and speech (speech discrimination) even with sound presented at adequate intensity levels for maximum understanding.

(6) Additional hearing dysfunctions coded within this group of hearing difficulties included one man referred to above who was *unable to localize sound source* (code 266), and two (2) men with added demonstrable organic hearing impairment (code 267) defined as tinnitus (head noises such as hissing, ringing, roar, etc., varying in degree of frequency and intensity).

Impairment of Voice Function

Normal human voice as defined by the Nomenclature of Communicative Disorders refers to ". . . the auditory experience of phonation which is culturally appropriate for communication." [3]

(1) In the area of *disorders of pitch,* two (2) priests coded 202, were evaluated as having a pitch level too high for sex and age. Pitch level referring to the central tendency of pitch around which the individual's inflectional and intonational variations habitually occur.

(2) *Disorder of loudness,* code 204, inadequate level of intensity to voice, revealed one (1) mild clinical problem. Level is defined as the central tendency or average loudness characteristic of an individual's speech.

(3) One (1) person was evaluated as having an excessive level of loudness to voice (code 205) directly related to a long-term hearing problem with only fair self-monitoring ability to judge and maintain appropriate intensity levels for particular speech-listening situations.

(4) *Disorders of quality* associated with phonation revealed the following problems:

a) One (1) case of breathiness to voice coded as 212. b) Two (2) disorders of quality associated with resonance factors were detected. Analysis revealed one (1) problem of *mild hypernasality* or an abnormal participation of the nasal resonators during phonation and speech (code 214); one (1) *mild hyponasal* problem or lack of participation of nasal resonators during speech production (code 215).

Impairment of Speech Function

Normal speech was recognized and defined as the oral and verbal expression of language appropriate to the environment of the speaker and the listener. The term inappropriate used below is from the reference point of the listener.[4] Speech problems detected were essentially clinically mild problems indicating short term speech improvement supervision and guidance but with a detailed program for continued self-application.

(1) Six (6) impairments of articulation were detected ranging from several sound substitution errors due to *bilingual background* to mild *sound distortion problems* (code 270) affecting clear, precise sibilant productions. In three (3) instances, difficulty with sibilant sounds was judged to be directly related to severe high frequency hearing loss of long duration above 2000 cycles per second.

(2) Two (2) priests were evaluated with evidence of moderate inappropriate disfluencies or instances of inappropriate pauses and repetition of sounds and syllables in both reading and spontaneous speech situations. The latter problems closely resembled very mild stuttering but without evidence of the struggle symptoms facial contortions, forcing, or use of consistent avoidances such as word substitutions and circumlocution in the attempt to dodge or circumvent a true block or interruption during speech. The two instances detected manifest themselves for one of the men only during oral reading and for the other priest during prepared speeches for the practicum sessions. The latter difficulty was dramatically conveyed during the video-tape recording session. These problems were coded as 271 in the nomenclature of communicative disorders.

PATTERNING OF GENERAL RECOMMENDATIONS

In the area of *hearing difficulties*, copies of report findings as well as copies of audiograms and speech audiometry results were provided each priest. Recommendations for practical assistance included definite suggestions for medical referral to the priest's physician and follow through in the immediate future. Practical suggestions included voluntary self-seating adjustments during critical listening situations, periodic hearing reevaluations to determine further loss in remaining hearing function, advice to seek speech and hearing conservation programs at speech and hearing clinics in the area of residence (names and addresses provided), suggestions for microphone practice and development of skills, possible consideration of amplification assistance following hearing testing reevaluations and medical directives, use of visual cues to reinforce loss of reduced hearing acuity, and prepared and distributed material covering information on the hearing apparatus and functions of the mechanism with aspects of mild to moderate defects.

Voice problems in all instances were advised to seek examination by otolaryngologists to rule out possible organic factors (one priest was scheduled for and received medical attention during the workshop period because of recent trauma to the voice mechanism). All priests were advised to seek voice consultation and training in their areas of residence. Card files were prepared giving exercises and appropriate references to assist self-training and follow through before guidance could be obtained. Practical techniques in intonation and intensity regulation were demonstrated and applied during the days of the remaining practica sessions with suggested reference materials for continued work following the workshop.

Speech problems were given direct therapy in identification and initial production of substituted or distorted sound units by means of a monophonic dual-track tape recorder using the concept of an appropriate model for comparison with their own mildly impaired sounds. Listings of personnel and agencies in speech and hearing in their area of residence were provided. Techniques of practice were emphasized during workshop proceedings and typed and distributed to the men by mail after the close of the workshop program.

MULTIPLE IMPAIRMENTS

Some of the priests evaluated evidenced more than one impaired function of the communication processes (speech, hearing, voice). A listing of those with more than one impaired function is given below:

Number of Priests	Functions Impaired
3	Voice, Speech
3	Voice, Hearing
2	Voice, Speech, Hearing
2	Speech, Hearing

These men presented particular problems in both classification and, most important, in direct consultation, immediate therapy, and long-range planning. All are planned to be carefully followed up by detailed correspondence with additional aspects of report findings to professional personnel in speech pathology and audiology in the priest's community.

FOOTNOTES

[1] *Rehabilitation Codes: Development and Field Testing of an Operational Tool for Serial Recording.* Special Project RD-788, Office of Vocational Rehabilitation, 1961-1964.

[2] *Rehabilitation Codes: Proceedings of the Workshop on Nomenclature of Communicative Disorders,* 1962, p. 18.

[3] *Ibid.,* p. 17.

[4] *Ibid.,* p. 21.

6 j